SATAN'S
CHILDREN

Also by Dr. Robert S. Mayer
Through Divided Minds

SATAN'S CHILDREN

Case Studies in Multiple Personality

DR. ROBERT S. MAYER

WITHDRAWN

G. P. PUTNAM'S SONS
New York

G. P. Putnam's Sons
Publishers Since 1838
200 Madison Avenue
New York, NY 10016

Library of Congress Cataloging-in-Publication Data

Mayer, Robert Stanley.
Satan's children : case studies in multiple personality /
Robert S. Mayer.
p.   cm.
ISBN 0-399-13627-4
1. Multiple personality—Etiology—Case studies.   2. Satanism—
Psychological aspects—Case studies.   3. Child abuse—Psychological
aspects—Case studies.   I. Title.
RC569.5.M8M388   1991   90-27385   CIP
616.85′236—dc20

Printed in the United States of America

1   2   3   4   5   6   7   8   9   10

This book is printed on acid-free paper.
∞

Acknowledgments

IN writing this book I incurred many debts to friends, relatives and colleagues who gave generously of their time, experience and wisdom. Among those I wish now to thank are:

Rena Rogge, research librarian at Kean College of New Jersey, for the many bibliographical computer searches she conducted, and my chairman, Professor Lawrence K. Zimmer, who helped temporarily free me from my teaching responsibilities so I could write.

Steven Gutkin and Beth and David Smith, who painstakingly read the manuscript, chapter by chapter.

Colin A. Ross, M.D., director of the Dissociative Disorders Clinic at St. Boniface General Hospital in Winnipeg, Canada, and Candace Orcett, Ph.D., and Judith Pearson, Ph.D., both associates at the Masterson Institute in New York City, for their encouragement and suggestions.

Arnold D. Richards, M.D., training and supervising analyst at the New York Psychoanalytic Institute, for helping me resolve the many emotional reactions I had while working with these patients.

Reese Markewich, M.D., a psychiatrist in New York City, for his valuable advice.

Arlene Levine, Ph.D., a psychologist in New York City and my sounding board, and George Ganaway, M.D., di-

6 ACKNOWLEDGMENTS

rector of the Ridgeview Center for Dissociative Disorders in Smyrna, Georgia, for his patience and insights during our many long talks about ritual abuse.

Colleagues across the country, including Richard Kluft, M.D., director of the Dissociative Disorders Program at the Institute of Pennsylvania Hospital; Robert Benjamin, M.D., medical director at Northwestern Institute in Suburban Philadelphia; and Roberta Sacks, Ph.D., director of training at the Dissociative Disorders Unit, Rush Presbyterian St. Luke's Medical Center, Chicago, who advised me from time to time on these cases.

Lisa Wager, my editor, for her skill and sensitivity in shaping this manuscript and for her faith in me.

And Laura, for her devotion and strength.

To my patients

Contents

9

10   CONTENTS

SATAN'S
CHILDREN

Introduction

MY parents created an over-achieving neurotic cursed with an unhappy personality but blessed with a determination to change it. This led me from college to business, back to academia and then through psychoanalysis to nearly two decades as a therapist trying to help others as I helped myself.

But I hadn't been a therapist long before I concluded that something was lacking in my new field, and so my search continued. I traveled from New York to Arizona to Washington State to Florida to Vermont to California. I was especially drawn to those who disagreed with the orthodoxy in which I was trained. Why? Because it did not offer the solution.

My travels and my studies opened my mind and left me with an array of analytic techniques that proved invaluable about 12 years ago when, after years of therapy that was at best mildly successful, a patient named Toby suddenly "switched" into another personality before my eyes. In an instant, this 32-year-old woman, whose day-to-day complaints filled our sessions, was transformed into what appeared to be a five- or six-year-old child who looked up at me and in a small and startling voice said, "Hi, I'm Beth." Then she stuck her thumb in her mouth.

Rather than concluding that she was psychotic and having her admitted to a hospital, as my conventional training told me to do, I listened to her and I talked to her and I worked with her and I learned from her. Soon I met five other personalities who lived within Toby, including Anna, who was about the same age as Toby but slightly depressed; Morgan, who appeared to be a boisterious teen-aged girl, and Julia, a shy flower child. Toby's affliction, multiple personality disorder, is now accepted by most of my colleagues in the therapeutic profession. But back then, many therapists were skeptical, and a good portion of those who weren't so skeptical considered multiple personality disorder quite rare. I had never been taught about multiplicity in any of my classes, nor was it mentioned in any of the texts I read during my training. My only knowledge of the disorder came from Flora Rheta Schreiber's best-selling book, *Sybil*, the story of a woman with 16 personalities, which I had read years earlier but did not take very seriously.

When I told my analytic supervisor about Toby's behavior, he told me that she was undoubtedly faking as a way of resisting treatment. I fired him—I'm sure he thought I was resisting—and sought out others who had gone before me: Dr. Cornelia Wilbur, Sybil's analyst; Dr. Ralph Allison, who wrote a wonderful book on multiplicity, *Minds in Many Pieces*; Dr. Milton Erickson, who showed me how hypnosis could be used to treat the disorder, and Dr. Judi-Ann Densen-Gerber, who founded Odyssey House, a treatment center for drug addicts, many of whom were also multiples. I asked questions. I studied. I came to believe that multiple personality disorder, far from being rare, was distressingly common, a consequence of another distressingly common problem, child abuse.

For a young person, this abuse, especially if it comes at the hands of a parent, is usually overwhelming. To survive, some children dissociate, which is a fancy psychiatric term for forgetting. The horror and the pain are placed in a compartment of the mind that is sealed off from normal consciousness.

But sometimes, somehow, that part can take on a life of its own. It can even become a separate personality inside the child. Repeated abuse can create additional internal personalities, or make the existing ones more complex, just as a normal personality becomes richer with experience. There is apparently no limit to the number of these personalities that can be formed.

These alter personalities help the child survive, becoming a protective shield from trauma so awful as to be nearly unimaginable. But a separate, independent personality living inside someone's body can be quite a handicap.

The treatment of multiple personality disorder is simple, at least theoretically. The therapist helps the patient pry open the lid of the psychic container and the memory of the traumatic episode is freed, becoming disarmed in the process. In practice, though, treating multiples is a long and difficult process. After all, patients have gone to great lengths to forget these episodes, and now the therapist must not only make them remember but actually sense and feel and re-experience the traumas, for that is the only way to truly free them. This means I have to take patients on a guided trip back into the hell of their childhoods.

It took years to recover the youth Toby had so carefully locked away. But eventually we discovered all the abuse she suffered, which included a rape at age five by a neighbor and vicious beatings by her mother.

After a memory is liberated, the alter personality created to contain it is no longer needed, so it must be merged into the host personality. Toby, like other multiples, was emotionally attached to her alters. They were her friends, even though they sometimes complicated her life. It was slow going, especially at first.

While I was treating Toby, I began to have consultations with other therapists in the same dilemma, and I began to see other patients with multiple personality disorder. Soon I founded a local professional organization, the Association for the Study of Dissociative Disorders, to study the syndrome and train therapists to work with patients who were multiples. In 1987 I wrote *Through Divided Minds*, the story of how I treated Toby and several other similarly afflicted patients. My practice grew. My techniques became refined. I was getting cases that involved more serious abuse, and more complex internal worlds, but to my immense satisfaction, my techniques were effective and for the most part these patients, many of whom had already been seen by five or six therapists, got better.

Then, gradually, a different kind of multiple personality patient began turning up in my office, reporting even more disturbing experiences than the ones to which I had become accustomed. These patients, usually but not always young women, claimed to have been abused ritually, by organized groups that practiced Satanism. While hardly the majority of my practice, these patients haunted me. The stories they told me were beyond anything I had ever heard or read about in the professional literature.

The following is an account of events that occurred in my psychiatric practice. The cases are based on true incidents. The stories related here were told to me by patients. But to ensure their privacy and their safety I have made changes. I have altered aspects of their identities and circumstances. Sometimes, I have grafted a part of one patient's identity or history onto another. This camouflaging is so extensive that no patient can be recognized.

Still, the dialogue presented here and my reflections on the cases are how I remembered them, to the best of my ability. The major characters have read the manuscript and approved its veracity. They hope that by telling their story, others may be helped. And, of course, I hope so, too.

Chapter 1

NED

He was late. I was worried.

I hadn't worried so much about a tardy patient since I was just starting out, an inexperienced analyst who was nonetheless terribly impressed with his skills. In those days, when a patient was late, I would usually assume I had done something wrong during the previous session. I remember talking about this with my supervising analyst. He listened calmly—nonjudgmentally, in the argot of our profession— and then observed as gently as possible that I must think of myself as very powerful indeed to have such an effect on a patient, especially a patient I had not been seeing for very long.

From then on, whenever a patient was late I tended to regard it as a sign of resistance, the desire to avoid the unpleasant issues that we were stirring up in therapy. In other words, it was the patient's fault, not mine. I would wait 15 minutes, then phone my tardy client. "Hi, this is Dr. Mayer," I would say, usually to an answering machine. "Don't we have an appointment now?" That would at least get the patient thinking about the implications of the absence.

I sat back in my imitation leather chair and thought about today's missing patient, which was only fair, since he would be paying for my time whether he showed up or not. Soon I drifted into a terrible fantasy: he had hanged himself. And his family was suing me for malpractice. Who would defend me? Was my insurance paid up? Someone with a degree on the wall from an analytic institute should not have such thoughts. After indulging myself a bit longer, I picked up the phone and dialed my patient's number. It rang five times, and I hung up.

Damn, I thought to myself. I don't need this. Not today. Not on a Friday, in a lovely patch of Indian summer that was likely to be the last warmth of the year before autumn turned serious. My wife and I had monitored the long range forecast on the Weather Channel all week and concluded that this would probably be the last weekend we would have to work on our sailboat. It had arrived from the Far East just a few months before, a gleaming, custom-designed craft that, to my great irritation, had a mast that was off center and a few small leaks. After they were fixed, the boat would still need the usual cleaning, waxing and fine-tuning. But I didn't really mind that part. In fact, I looked forward to it. Sitting in a chair all week makes me yearn for physical activity. Psychotherapy often seems an unending process, like painting the Golden Gate Bridge, and there is nothing like a freshly varnished teak toe-rail to deeply instill a sense of accomplishment and a well-earned feeling of fatigue.

The thought of my absent patient brought me back from sea. Where was he? Thirty minutes to go in his session.

Let's call him Ned. He was a friend of a friend of my wife's sister. She had referred him to me two years earlier.

Ned seemed like the last person one would think needed psychiatric help. Born and raised in an Illinois college town, he was tall and maybe a little too thin, although this was more than compensated by his sandy-haired, All-American looks. Ned was very bright and had a relaxed charm that made him easy to be with. He was the type of young man that I had looked up to in high school. I remember being amazed when he told me he had few friends and was quite shy with women.

Ned had worked after high school and on weekends to accumulate spending money for college. The son of a physician, he had been a pre-med student at the University of California at Berkeley, graduating summa cum laude. But a strange thing happened as he headed back to the Midwest for medical school in a new red Toyota that was a graduation present from his parents. He kept driving east and did not stop until he reached New York City. He gave up his place in medical school, rented an apartment in the East Village, sold the Toyota and took a job driving a van for a private school. He came to see me a little while later because, he said, he was lonely.

Ned was not sure why he had taken this sudden detour from a path that had been so carefully laid out, and he did not seem to want to talk about it. Our early discussions focused on his social life, such as it was. For such a handsome man in a city with about three times as many women as men his age, the odds were with him. But Ned did not date. He said he was uncomfortable in the artificial environs of the city's singles scene. He found it intolerable even to make eye contact, much less actually converse, with a woman. On those infrequent occasions when he would muster his courage and force himself to go into a bar, he would usually just sit by himself for a little while and then walk out, feeling deflated. When a woman would approach him, which was not uncommon, he would become tongue-tied. Once, after weeks of encouragement, I convinced him to go to a dance, arbitrarily pick out a woman and introduce himself. Just do it as an experiment, I urged. And he did. Do you know what happened? She turned her back and walked away.

Ned still had sexual needs, of course, and to satisfy them

he created a fantasy world out of the endless supply of pornography available in the seedy stores around Times Square. When I asked him whether he ever felt afraid on his nocturnal travels through the blighted and dangerous neighborhood, he would reply that it was the only place where he felt truly comfortable. "His people" were there, he told me, referring to the downcast, the rejected, the losers attracted to the area. He would tour the book and video shops, pay to spend a few moments talking to a semi- or fully-naked lady in a booth or watch a live sex show before heading home, stopping on the way for Twinkies or Mallomars, his favorites.

Back in his one-room apartment on Avenue C, in a part of New York that is home to people with oddly cut and colored hair, motorcycle gang members, drug sellers and users and others simply unable to afford the exorbitant rents in better neighborhoods, Ned would get stoned on marijuana, insert a porno tape into his VCR, break out his goodies and drift off into a world of his own, imagining himself as the star of the movies unfolding before him. His evenings would end when, in a hazy, drugged state, he would masturbate, timing his orgasm to the action on the screen. Then he would sleep.

Ned sometimes used a second VCR to copy his favorite scenes onto one of several carefully edited master tapes filled with the material that titillated him the most. I was amazed at how he focused his creative energies in the service of this obsession, and at how he was able to build and maintain such strong relationships with the two-dimensional images on the screen. He knew all the actors' names. He had preferences for certain directors. He bought magazines that reviewed the films and kept up on the latest porno-industry gossip.

• Ned's life was like Styrofoam—it filled space but was in essence empty. But I listened to his video adventures dispassionately, so that he would continue to share them with me. It did not take me long to reach a hypothesis on the case: Ned was an addict. In his case, he was addicted not to cocaine, heroin or even the marijuana he used so regularly, but rather to pornography. He could not sleep unless he got his video fix.

Whether it involves drugs or pornography, addictive behavior often masks other, more fundamental problems. Remove the addiction and these underlying problems surface. My training in classical psychoanalytic theory led me to suspect that behind Ned's obsession with pornography was a strong Oedipal attachment to his mother. Freudian theory holds that when boys are three to six years of age they want to sexually possess their mothers. Fearing the wrath of their father, however, they push this urge down. Later, at a more appropriate age, these feelings rise up again and become the basis for the mature love of an appropriate mate.

I believed that Ned never outgrew his Oedipal, libidinous feelings about his mother. At the time when he was supposed to transfer them to a proper object, he didn't. Real women just could not compare to the idealized image he had of his mother. As a result, Ned relied on fantasy. His refusal to go to medical school, I believed, reflected an Oedipal fear of his father, a fear of competing with this man who was already a successful physician. Ned's way off the horns of this dilemma was to jump, which is what he did when he drove to New York.

What caused Ned to become stuck in his Oedipal phase? One possibility was that he had been overstimulated at an important developmental stage by his mother. Some sort of voyeuristic or incestuous relationship with her would have accounted for his behavior now.

These suspicions arose from the case of a man I had treated with a problem similar to Ned's. He would spend many evenings relaxing in a big leather easy chair in the darkened living room of his high-rise apartment, a glass of cognac by his side, leisurely scanning the neighboring windows through a pair of powerful binoculars, hoping to catch a glimpse of a woman undressing or a couple making love. When we analyzed his voyeurism, I learned that while he was going through puberty his mother would often dress in front of him. That she was being seductive was beyond doubt. She would call him into her room saying she wanted to talk, then slowly put her stockings on, smoothing them up and down her leg, straightening the seams—this was in the 1940s—and fastening them to garters. Sometimes, she would get up and go to the closet to change her clothes, carefully turning her back to her son at the moment a bra or some other undergarment came off. Decades later, my patient still remembered seeing a flash of breast or some other forbidden part.

After he reached puberty, this patient found pictures of his mother naked. It seemed likely to me that they had been left by her for him to find, just as some believe Jocasta encouraged her son Oedipus. My patient told me he would look at the pictures while he masturbated, although he first cut off her head.

When I tried to talk to Ned about his mother, he professed not to have a very good memory of her, or any other aspect of his childhood. He preferred to stay in the present, complaining in session after session about his social life. Each time I tried to get him to focus on his upbringing, Ned would angrily yank me back, claiming not to see how events long ago could be causing his problems now. I decided to follow a time-honored analytic rule and simply wait him out. If he wanted to discuss the present, that is what we would discuss.

Not that we made much progress on that front. Ned could not cope with a woman who was not on videotape, and all my efforts to help him change were met with the same opposition that greeted my attempts to get him to talk about his past. When I pointed out that his masturbation was sidetracking him from going out and meeting women, he would sadly agree. But he would argue that whenever he tried to stop masturbating, the tension would build and build until he was forced to give in. It was the only thing that made him calm, he insisted.

I wanted Ned to allow the feelings that the addictive behavior was suppressing to surface. That was the only way he could resolve them. But Ned said he just wasn't strong enough. After a while, I realized that my encouragement was only confirming his own feelings of weakness, making him feel worse.

Well, if you can't go up the mountain one way, try another. Staying in the present to minimize his resistance, I refocused our sessions on Ned's potential medical career. I needed to help him find something that he could be proud of, something that would build self-esteem and eventually enable him to give up the considerable pleasures of his private world for the pain he would initially find in the real one. So we talked about why he chose not to go to medical school and what was stopping him from reapplying. He told me he was afraid he might fail and that he doubted that he would ever be as good a physician as his father. As an undergraduate, Ned told me, all he did was study. That was how he had earned his A average and admission to medical school. But it took a total effort and he doubted he would be able to maintain that discipline now. By the time he left Berkeley, he said, he was burned out. He was sure the competition in medical school would be even keener, and he feared he would never get through it.

Like water on stone, therapy gradually wore away at him. Perhaps Ned didn't really want to practice medicine, but some part of him certainly wanted to prove that he could. After I had been seeing him for about a year, he applied to and was accepted at a medical school, winning a scholarship and money for living expenses and a medical insurance policy, which let him continue therapy, though only once a week.

I was starting to feel as though I was turning the corner on Ned's case. He had begun classes a few weeks earlier, just after his 23rd birthday, and the pressure of school, I figured, would leave him little time to wander through Times Square.

Ned's 45 minutes were just about up, and he still had not arrived. He had never missed an appointment before. I could not even recall an instance when he had been late.

I heard the doorman ring, alerting me that my next patient was here. I had no choice but to push Ned from my mind.

BY evening, all my thoughts were on my boat and the battle I was having with Mao Ta, its Taiwanese builder. My lawyer told me I could sue and win. Collecting, though, would be another matter. I was so agitated that I ignored the phone when it rang several times during the evening. I saw the calls when I checked my answering machine before turning in. There were no messages, though, only hang-ups, which I distractedly dismissed as wrong numbers.

As I was falling asleep the phone rang again. This time I picked it up.

"This is the international operator. I have a collect call from a Ned in San Juan, Puerto Rico, for Dr. Robert Mayer. Will you accept?"

Puerto Rico?

"Ned?"

"I'm sorry to call you like this—I mean so late—but I'm in trouble."

He sounded sheepish. Unable to maintain professional neutrality, I heard myself ask, "What happened? What are you doing in Puerto Rico?"

"I don't know. I just woke up here this morning. I didn't know where I was. The last thing I remembered was that I was in school. Then I woke up in this hotel room in San Juan. I didn't know where I was, so I went downstairs and saw that the newspapers were in Spanish. And that five days have gone by. Look, I feel really funny asking you this, but I don't have any money and I don't know how I'm going to get home. Can you send me a plane ticket or something? I'll pay you back as soon as I get to New York. I can't ask my parents. I just can't deal with them. And, uh, Dr. Mayer, I lost time again."

Lost time again. I had heard that phrase before.

I told Ned not to worry. I would wire him money for a ticket in the morning, and we would talk about it all when he got back.

Chapter 2

FUGUE

I almost always let patients start the session. But when I finally found myself looking across my office at Ned, I could not resist beginning.

"So, what happened?"

"I told you on the phone about how I found myself in Puerto Rico," Ned said somewhat shortly. After a pause, he added: "I don't know what else to say."

"Has this ever happened to you before? Have you ever found yourself in a place and not known how you got there?"

"Yes."

"Well, why didn't you tell me about it before this?"

"I wanted to, but I was afraid that you would think I was crazy and put me in a hospital. Besides, most of the time I managed not to think about it."

"How are you able not to think about these things?" I asked, growing more concerned about him.

"I just don't. I think about other things, I guess."

Ned was just sitting there, silent and passive. I knew I would have to take the lead.

26

"Do you have things in your apartment—clothes, for instance—that you don't remember buying?"

"Yes."

"Do you hear voices in your head?"

"Doesn't everybody?"

"Can you remember what was happening to you before you woke up in San Juan?"

"The last thing I knew, it was Monday morning. We woke up, then went through our usual morning routine and went to school. It was anatomy lab day. We had waited a month for our lab assignments and they finally came in. I was assigned to share a cadaver with another student, Deborah. I was a little nervous—a dead person would be lying on a table in front of me. I guess I was worried it might be a woman. I was worried about my voyeurism. It would be, you know, naked, and I didn't know whether I could deal with that, not in front of Deborah."

Ned's alternate use of the first person plural "we" increased my confidence in the tentative diagnosis that was shaping up in my mind. I wondered why I hadn't picked up on that before. Maybe he had only begun using it today.

"When we got to school, I put on the lab gown, went into the lab and listened to the instructor explain what we were going to do. Deborah said I should start. I picked up the blade and inserted it into the body and then all of a sudden I started to have a horrible—I don't know what to call it, it was like a dream, just this overpowering feeling. I don't know how to explain it, Dr. Mayer, except that I felt—I was convinced—something terrible had happened. That I had done something terrible. That I had killed somebody. I know that sounds crazy. I'm not sure. It was clear then, but now it's a little fuzzy. But I remember being so scared I was shaking. I ran out of there. I just had to get out. I don't really know what happened next, except that I woke up in the hotel."

"In San Juan?"

"In San Juan."

Ned was pale and sweaty.

"God, it's awful to not know where you are. It was dark out. I just lay there for about an hour, in bed. Not moving. Finally, I got up and went downstairs. I saw a newspaper in a rack by the desk. It was in Spanish. I saw that the date was a Friday. That meant I had lost five days. I walked around for a while and then went back to the room. That's when I called you."

The lost time, the reluctance to open up about his past, the sense of distrust—it was all adding up. Ned, I was almost completely convinced, was suffering from multiple personality disorder. He was split into pieces, into different personalities that were sharing one body.

How did I miss it? I'm supposed to be an expert on multiple personality disorder. I had even written a book about it. But multiples do not trust easily. They almost always test their therapists for a long time before they allow themselves to show any symptoms. This stems from the cause of the illness: severe trauma in childhood, usually physical or sexual abuse that is most often inflicted before the age of five and sometimes continues for years. Typically, the victimizer is a family member, often a mother or father or both. Even if only one parent is directly involved, the other is usually a silent collaborator, unwilling or unable to believe or help the child, perhaps for fear of splitting the family. And so the child is forced to rely on his own scant resources. Some dissociate, which means they essentially banish the painful experiences from conscious awareness. One way to do this is to create an additional personality to absorb the pain. *I wasn't hurt; she was.* As a result, multiples have an extraordinary ability to push things from their mind, to "think about it tomorrow," as Scarlett O'Hara said.

In some cases, the child does not have to suffer a trauma, but merely witness it. Chris Sizemore, the Eve of *Three Faces of Eve*, became a multiple after watching a man cut in half in a lumberyard. However, an important factor in the development of multiple personality disorder is the absence of a sympathetic adult to help a young victim make sense of a disturbing experience. During World War II in London, many children were exposed to the Blitz but did not develop multiple personalities because their parents were there to explain the bombing.

Alternate personalities are created unconsciously. No one fully understands the mechanism involved, but the process seems analogous to the childhood game of hot potato. The pain is too hot for the central personality, so it forms another personality to handle it. The rudiments of multiplicity can be seen in the many normal children who invent imaginary playmates. With people suffering from multiple personality disorder, these alternate personalities take on lives of their own. Over the years, they can absorb additional traumatic experiences and become fuller, more complex, more lifelike. Or sometimes continuing abuse leads to the creation of additional alter personalities. Once the machinery is in place, personalities also can be formed to fulfill difficult or unpleasant functions as well as contain pain. I once treated a patient who hated to clean her house, so she created another personality who tidied up on Thursdays. This personality hated to do windows, but there was still another personality who came out once a month to scrub the panes.

Sometimes the multiplicity machine goes out of control, and what once was adaptive becomes pathological. That is what happened when Ned found himself in a strange hotel room. Yet even though multiples are experts at forgetting, there is always some part of them that retains all the memories, even the most painful ones. Therapy, when it is successful, reaches this part, accessing the memories and making conscious the unconscious.

Three decades ago there was much skepticism within the psychiatric community about multiple personality disorder, and even today some therapists consider it extremely rare. But many others, citing what is generally believed to be

a far higher incidence of child abuse than has previously
been acknowledged, believe multiplicity, too, is far more
common.

I had been a member of the skeptical camp, until I took
on a patient named Toby. She was about 28 and had been
having difficulties adjusting to life in New York. After I had
seen Toby for about a year, she developed a strange
symptom—she sometimes found it difficult to talk, especially during our sessions. When we investigated this, Toby
told me she felt as if there were two hands around her neck.

For weeks nothing I said or did seemed to work. Then,
almost in desperation, I remembered a technique I learned
from Fritz Perls, a therapist with whom I had studied years
earlier at the Esalen Institute in Big Sur, California, where
he had established himself as the founder of Gestalt therapy. I asked Toby to "become" the hands, by projecting
thoughts and feelings onto them, as a child might do with a
stuffed animal. After some initial resistance, and more encouragement from me, she started to repeat, "I am the
hands around my throat that are preventing me from . . ."
But she never finished the sentence. Her eyes closed, her
body shuddered and before my eyes she was transformed
from an adult into a childlike presence. She had a child's
tiny, hesitant voice, a child's fidgety mannerisms and a
child's bewilderment at being in a doctor's office. She
wasn't acting, either. She couldn't have been that good.
Toby had switched into another personality who, I later
learned, was a precocious five-year-old named Beth. I remember feeling a chill rise up through my body. It was
almost spiritual, as if something or someone had taken
possession of Toby. Only I didn't believe in possession.

Somehow I managed to stay calm and soon found myself
talking to this childlike woman as if she actually were a five-
year-old. Eventually, I met Toby's other internal personalities: the highly intelligent Anna, who was about the
same age as Toby and seemed to be in charge of the group;
Morgan, an outgoing teenager, and Julia, who was shy and

sweet. After about 20 minutes, I began to worry about how I would switch my patient back to the one who walked into the office. I told Beth it had been nice to meet her, assured her that we would talk again and asked to speak to Toby. She said good-bye, closed her eyes and shuddered. When her eyes opened, I knew Toby had returned.

We analysts have analysts of our own—more experienced supervisors we consult about difficult cases, just as priests consult their bishops. So I went to my supervisor and told him about Toby. Multiple personality disorder is very rare, he told me. Toby was simply making it up to get attention.

"Okay, let's assume it was resistance," I agreed. "What should I do about it?"

"Tell it to go away," he replied curtly.

Well, I tried to make it go away, but it didn't. All I ended up doing was angering Toby and the rest of her personalities. There were even accusations that I was trying to "kill" them. I quickly decided I had no option but to accept their existence and work with each of them as I would any patient. Eventually, I found other therapists with experience treating patients with multiple personality disorder and, with their help, I was able to merge Toby's alter personalities into her main personality one by one.

Like Toby, multiples generally complain of other problems until they are absolutely certain a therapist is truly sympathetic. It takes them quite a while to build up enough confidence to be able to talk about the other people living in their bodies, other people who, at any moment, can take control and move the entire collection of personalities to, say, Puerto Rico, where a person can wake up, having lost nearly a week, and not know how he got there.

Although I had tried during my sessions with Ned to convince him to give up his nightly pornographic ritual, I had carefully avoided expressing a judgment on the way he chose to live. While his activities were preventing him from forming healthy relationships, he wasn't hurting anyone

except himself. My respectful approach must have gradually given Ned confidence in me. Thinking back on some of
our sessions, I realized that he might have been so excru-
ciatingly explicit about his fantasy life to test me. And
perhaps by not showing revulsion or disapproval, I had
passed. The average patient with multiple personality disorder spends almost seven years with at least three therapists before he is correctly diagnosed. Ned and I were lucky.
His case had blossomed in less than two years.

I believed Ned had experienced some disturbing experience in childhood that had caused him to create an alternate personality to handle the pain. And something in the
anatomy lab must have reminded him of that original
trauma, freeing a long-buried memory. These memories are
like bubbles that cling to the side of a glass of seltzer. Tap
the glass and some of the bubbles rise to the surface and
burst. When the freed memory rose into Ned's consciousness, he instinctively protected himself as he did when he
was a child—he dissociated. He didn't need to create another personality, since another one already existed. All he
had to do was switch into it. It was this alternate personality, I believed, who took Ned far away from the
trauma—all the way to Puerto Rico.

"Can you tell me whether you noticed anything unusual
in the lab?" I asked Ned. "Whether anything there reminded you of something? Think carefully, Ned. What set
you off? What were you thinking?"

"I don't know. I get very anxious when I try to think
about it."

"Try to remember."

Ned was still unsure he wanted to make the effort. Then
he began again, tentatively.

"I am little. Everything looks big. I am in a strange room.
It's dark—no, it's dim. There are candles, lots of candles.
As I think about it, it's getting very hazy and far away. I'm
having trouble remembering. It starts to disappear as I talk,
and other things come in. I don't know if I can get it."

I had a technique that might help us, but I was almost afraid to suggest it. I knew what kind of reaction I was likely to get.

"Ned, what if I tried to hypnotize you so you could relax and get the memory back?"

"Hypnotize me?" Ned said. "I'm not sure."

It is a common response, even from a medical student. Hypnosis has an image problem. It has been used on too many stages and at too many parties. Although we still can't explain exactly how it works, hypnosis appears to be a simple, natural process that allows therapists to access their patients' unconscious, the repository of memories and experiences that determines so much of our behavior.

I think of hypnosis as a focused state of attention. We can see an entire picture or close in on just one part. We can listen to background noise or, with a little practice, isolate one of the sounds that comprise it, increasing its volume and diminishing that of the others. If the center of our attention is on some injury we have suffered, we will feel the pain. If we focus on the injury with more intensity, it will hurt more. If we shift our attention away from the injury, the pain will diminish. If our attention moves far enough away, the pain will disappear. We can do this inwardly also, letting the real world fade and focusing on thoughts or feelings or even on memories.

The expert who taught me the techniques of hypnosis, Milton Erickson, was a living example of its power. Erickson suffered from polio, two strokes and severe arthritis. He was in terrible and constant pain. But he would put himself into a trance each morning to dissociate from it, so he would be able to work with students in the afternoon.

"Ned, all of us go into trances naturally from time to time," I said, lowering my voice. "We just don't recognize them. Have you ever been reading a book and become so engrossed that you didn't hear it when someone called your name? Maybe it took them three tries before they were able to get your attention."

I got a wary nod.

"Or have you ever been so caught up in a movie that you forgot how crowded the theater was? Or even that you were in a theater? But if the movie was boring, then you had the opposite experience, right? You noticed that the seat was hard, or there wasn't enough legroom, or the person next to you was hogging the armrest."

He smiled for the first time all morning.

"Those are trance states. States of focused attention. Look, Ned, I can't hypnotize you. Nobody can. All I can do is help you do something that you already know how to do, but don't know that you know how to do it."

Now he looked at me as if I were the one who needed therapy.

"Look, you know how to get out of that chair. You know that you know how to do that. But can you tell me how you do it?"

He gave me another quizzical look.

"Which muscle do you move first to get up out of the chair? Is it a muscle in your neck? A muscle in your back? A muscle in your stomach? You aren't sure, are you Ned? Yet you know how to get up. You just don't know how you get up. That is what hypnosis is about, Ned. With your permission, I am going to teach you how to do it. How to do something that you can do, but you don't know you know how to do it."

By now my double-talk was having its intended effect. My slow, monotonous monologue had started to relax him. His expression had softened and his eyes were fluttering slightly. His breathing had slowed and deepened. With a little more double-talk from me, Ned was in a light trance.

This, too, confirmed my tentative diagnosis. Multiples are extremely hypnotizable. In fact, many of my colleagues believe that they go into self-hypnotic states when they create the alternate personalities.

To put Ned in a deeper trance, I decided to perform a formal hypnotic induction.

"Close your eyes, Ned. Let your body become comfortable."

He shifted slightly in his chair.

"If you hear sounds outside, you can listen to them or let them pass through your mind. You may even choose not to hear them at all. You will hear my voice. My voice will go with you wherever you go. You will always stay in contact with my voice.

"Very good," I said, gently rewarding him for his cooperation. "Now, I'm going to count from twenty to zero. As I do this, you will find yourself getting more and more relaxed, drifting into a state of complete relaxation. You might want to help it along by visualizing the numbers as I say them. They are being written on a sandy beach. Watch as one by one each number is erased by the waves and a new one appears."

By the time I got to six, Ned's shoulders were sagging. I finished counting, timing the last five numbers to the rhythm of his breathing. To make sure he was in a trance, I gave him a test.

"I'm going to place a balloon on your left wrist, Ned. You will notice it is gently tugging your arm into the air. That's right, it is gently lifting your arm up."

As I talked, his left arm slowly started to rise until it was stretched out in front of him.

"Now I am going to remove the balloon and your arm will gently float down to a comfortable position, resting on your leg."

It did. Reassured, I began my hypnotic investigation.

"Ned, place your hands on your thighs, so I can see them. That's good. Now let your body pick out a finger on your right hand to signify 'yes.' The finger will designate itself with a gentle movement up in the air."

Ned's right index finger rose and twitched slightly.

"Now, let your body pick out a finger on the same hand to signify 'no.' "

This time his thumb moved.

"Now, Ned, I want you to let your body show me a sign to stop. You can use it if you want me to stop for any reason."

His right arm rose and he turned his palm toward me, like a traffic cop at an intersection.

I fixed the signs in my mind—right index finger was yes, thumb was no and palm was stop.

It was time for the question I had been waiting the whole session to ask. I was careful to phrase it impersonally, so as not to offend the alternate personalities I suspected dwelled within the young man before me.

"Are there other people living in Ned's body?"

His right index finger went up.

"Are there more than two?"

The right index finger went up again.

"Are there more than ten?"

The right index finger went up once more.

"More than twenty?"

Again, the answer was positive. I was starting to get nervous. More than 20 personalities sharing one body? There were only three faces of Eve.

"Can I talk to the personality who decided to go to Puerto Rico?"

Ned's body shuddered. His expression was momentarily clouded. Then his head turned to the left and his eyes opened. They had a different look about them now—brighter, almost mischievous.

"Hey. How're ya doing."

It was Ned's voice, but with a different inflection. He sounded much stronger, more self-assured.

"Who are you?"

"Steve. You know, as in Steve Martin. The comedian. My job is to lighten things up. And I know who you are. You're the craaaaaaaazy doctor. We've been watching you."

"Tell me how you got to Puerto Rico."

"On an airplane."

"I mean what happened that day? In the lab?"

"Excuuuuuuuusssse me. Are you always so serious?"

Steve must have noticed the frustration on my face. "Okay, okay, okaaaaaaaay. I was walking along on Broadway and all of a sudden I just felt the urge to get away and have some fun. So I decided to go play a little dice."

"Why Puerto Rico?" I asked.

"His father gambles so he has lots of connections with the casino crowd. They fly him and his mother on junkets. They took me along a few times. These high rollers, the casinos comp them, you know, pay all their expenses—plane, hotel suite, meals—because they know they will make it up at the tables. If they gamble a whole lot they can sometimes get their friends comped, too.

"So I called this guy who used to take Ned's father to Vegas and told him who I was and that I wanted to go to Puerto Rico for a few days and could he do that? He could and he did."

"Then what?"

"Well, I got to the hotel. It was right by the beach. I checked in and was told there was a five-thousand-dollar line of credit for me in the casino. A few minutes later, there was this knock on the door. When I opened it, there was this beautiful woman standing there. In a tight black dress. And the hiiiiiiiiighest heels.

"I asked her who she was and what she was there for, not that I couldn't guess. She said her name was Alice and that she had been sent to see me. She was comped, too."

Steve apparently suffered none of Ned's shyness with women.

"After we were through, we went downstairs. I shot craps. Won about a thousand dollars. Then we went shopping, Alice and me. For clothes. Resort wear, you know.

"We had a ball. Gambled. Drank. Danced. Ate. Caught some rays. At the end of two days, the comp ended. But I didn't feel like going home yet, so I checked into a cheaper hotel in the old city. But in a couple of days my winnings ran out, so I went away and Ned came back."

"And Alice?" I was trying hard not to show my disbelief.

"Oh, she had left by then."

I talked to Steve for a few more moments, then told him that I wanted to meet the person who was there before he found himself on Broadway. Steve waved his right hand in farewell. Ned's eyes closed and his body slumped in his chair. Then his back straightened with a jolt. His eyes were open wide now, and his lower jaw jutted forward. He had an amazed, even frightened, expression. Suddenly Ned—or whoever was in control—jumped out of the chair, ran to a corner of the office, crouched his lanky, six-foot frame between a file cabinet and the couch, and he started to scream in a high voice. It took me a few moments to make out what he was saying.

"Don't kill the baby! Please! Don't kill the baby!"

From swaggering to screaming in a few seconds. The change was so abrupt I did not know what to think, much less what to do. The only thing I could figure was that I was now dealing with a child, just like in that session with Toby. Trying to keep my own composure, I mustered my most soothing voice and pressed into service one of the teddy bears I kept in the office to help quiet patients. Gradually, he calmed down, although I couldn't coax him from the corner. Soon, I learned that I was now talking with Terry, who seemed to be about six or seven years old.

"Tell me what is frightening you, Terry."

"I don't want to kill the baby."

"I don't understand."

"I don't want to kill the baby. I don't want to kill the baby."

He went on and on like this, clutching my little bear and sobbing. He was still in the corner. I realized there was no possibility of meaningful communication with Terry, so I decided to try to send him back inside. Terry looked grateful as he closed his eyes.

"Let me talk to Ned," I said, not knowing who to expect next.

The body stiffened. I hoped Ned was back.

"That's right, Ned. Stay in the trance. Now please move back over to the chair."

He got up slowly and walked back to the seat opposite me. Meanwhile, I thought back to the beginning of the session and how, when Ned talked about the anatomy lab, he had a feeling that he had killed someone. Is that what Terry was babbling about? I decided to see if I could find a connection.

"Do you remember what happened to you in the lab last week?"

"Yes," he said, starting to tremble. I had jarred a bubble loose and it was heading for the surface.

It would be easier for Ned, I realized, if I could separate the feelings from the memory, so that he could recall the event dispassionately, as if in the third person. Dr. Bennett Braun, of Rush Presbyterian St. Luke's Medical Center in Chicago, has a model of dissociation he calls BASK, an acronym for the components of normal experience— behavior, affect, sensations and knowledge. Dr. Braun believes that any one of these can be split off from the others and recalled separately. In this case, I felt it would be better if Ned tried to access only his knowledge of the event and left the feelings buried inside. Fortunately, Ned was still in a trance, which would make it easier.

"Ned, tell me what happened," I said. "You can remember it, but you do not have to remember the feelings. You can bring the memory out and leave the feelings behind. Just imagine that you can see it, like on a television screen."

That is all it took.

"I remember being in the lab," Ned began. "I am wearing a white coat. I see myself going over to the cadaver. I pick up the scalpel and insert it into the body. And then there is this terrible memory."

"What was it, Ned?"

"I am smaller. Younger. I am in a place where I had been before. It is big and dark, with lots of candles. There are other children there, too. Only they are in cages. And I am in a cage."

"A cage?"

"Yes, like on a farm. But smaller, with solid tops and bottoms and wire mesh all around. We have to sit in order to fit in them."

This was hard for me to accept, but I let him keep going.

"There are men there, men with horns, and there is a big table in the center, with two large chairs behind it."

"With horns?"

"Yes, with horns coming out of their heads. Wearing robes. Black robes."

"Horns and robes? What happens in this place?"

"The men form a circle. They hold hands and dance. They chant over and over again. 'Hail Satan. We are servants of Satan. Hail Satan.' Then they take me out of the cage, pick up this silver goblet and empty it over me. It has blood in it. It feels sticky."

There was a look of disgust on Ned's face. And, I am sure, a look of disbelief on mine.

"The leader gets out of the chair and pours more blood on a baby lying on the table. He takes a long knife and puts it in my hand and says, 'We offer this child to Satan as a sacrifice. May Satan's will be done; may Satan accept this sacrifice.' "

There was nothing to do except stay with Ned and see where he was going.

"The leader puts the knife in my hand, gets behind me, pushes me to the table. He holds my hands on the knife, raises it up and plunges it into the baby's chest. The blood spurts up.

"Then the leader takes the knife out of my hand, reaches into the chest and pulls out something. It's the heart. He holds it up in the air and shows it to the others. 'Hail Satan, master of the earthly world,' he says. Then he cuts off a piece of it, eats it, and gives pieces to the other men and me."

"Then what?"

Ned lowered his voice now. "He made me eat it."

There was a pause that seemed very long. I just looked at him.

"All the men form a circle and dance around me. And they chant. 'Hail Satan, hail child of Satan, hail prince of Satan.' Then they place me on my back in the center of the circle. They take my clothes off and rub oil all over my body. The women come over, and they touch me everywhere. I am ashamed, because it felt good.

"Then I was taken into the next room. My mother and father were there. They washed me, gave me clean clothes and took me home."

Ned was silent for a moment. He looked at me for the first time in a while.

"When I started to put the knife into the cadaver, that whole scene flashed into my head. It was just like it was happening. I couldn't stand it. So I ran out of the lab. The next thing I knew I was in that hotel. In Puerto Rico."

I still wasn't sure how this story and Steve's tale fit together, but from my experience with multiples I knew that such narratives often did not mesh smoothly. If you confront them about inconsistencies, however, they are apt to switch again, so I have gotten used to a certain amount of confusion.

"Okay, Ned, okay," I told him. "You've been through a lot for one day. Let yourself rest in the trance for a while."

I gave him a couple of minutes, while I thought about what I had heard. I was familiar with reports about victims of satanic cults. From time to time, I noticed items in the newspapers describing arrests of cult members. I also had heard stories from colleagues treating patients who claimed to have been cult victims. I once heard a police officer give a talk on satanic crimes at a conference of therapists. He said that police departments across the country were conducting seminars to train officers in how to recognize satanic elements in crimes. Ritual abuse, as it is known in psychiatric circles, had become quite controversial, as multiple personality disorder had been and, I guess, still is. Could Ned possibly have gone through anything as gruesome as he had described? And how could he have kept it bottled up all this time? Wasn't it more likely that it was just a terrible fantasy?

One thing was certain. Ned was totally shaken. I decided it would be best to try to help him forget this memory, at least for a while, before he left my office. We could always retrieve it later, after I had a chance to figure out what it meant.

Luckily, it's usually not a problem to make a good hypnotic subject forget something, especially something he has already forgotten. I told Ned that he would not remember anything that went on in the session after he came out of his trance. I was going to count from one to five, I told him, and by the time I was finished he would be fully awake.

When Ned emerged from the trance, his face was drawn, his mouth drooping and his blond hair damp with sweat. He looked as though he had a massive hangover. I told him to go home. I told him that we had done a lot of work while he was in the trance. He might feel foggy. His reflexes might not be as sharp as usual. I urged him to be extra careful going home and, once there, to go straight to bed. He could call me if he needed to. He nodded dully. Ned wasn't curious about what went on. Just dazed. This was a person, I thought to myself, who really wants to forget.

FOR days my wife and I had been looking forward to watching Fred and Ginger in *Top Hat.* But as I put the tape into our VCR that evening, I couldn't concentrate. I kept thinking about Ned and his weird memory—if it was a memory. After two decades as an analyst, I thought nothing could throw me. But how could anyone believe his tale of Satan worship and cannibalism?

I somehow wasn't surprised when the phone rang and I heard Ned's voice on the other end.

"I can't take it," he said intensely. "I can't take knowing that I murdered a child. My mind is filled with memories. It's like being inside one of those TV newsrooms, with monitors all around, each one with a different picture. I can't take it."

The hypnotic amnesia I had applied with such confidence clearly was not holding. He didn't forget.

"Can you come in tomorrow, so we can talk about it?"

"No. Not tomorrow. I can't wait."

"All right. If it's really an emergency, I can see you now."

"But I'm scared to go out of the house."

I decided to talk to him on the phone and see if I could help calm him, at least until the morning when he could come into the office.

"What are you doing now, Ned?"

"I'm watching TV. I thought it would distract me. But I don't have the sound on." He sounded like he was a million miles away.

"What are you watching."

"George C. Scott. *The Day of the Dolphin.* But it's better without the sound, because I can make up the dialogue."

There was a pause.

"Oh my God," said Ned sucking in his breath. "I looked at the clock to see what time it was and it just exploded. There are pieces all over the room."

As I was trying to decide what to do, he started to scream.

"My God, the people are coming out of the TV. They're here, in the room. With me."

"Just hold on, Ned," I said. "I'm coming right over. Just wait there for me. Don't do anything. Don't go anywhere."

Ned's apartment was only about a dozen blocks away. I must have been there in about 10 minutes. The front door to the tenement building was open so I went upstairs. The door to his apartment was locked. I knocked as hard as I could, but there was no answer. I knocked again. Then, on impulse, I put my shoulder against the door and shoved it with all the force that my 50-year-old body could muster. The door popped open and I was inside.

I looked around the room. It was furnished in student contemporary, with a battered couch and an upholstered easy chair. The television was still playing *The Day of the Dolphin.* In an alcove on the other side was a single bed. Ned was lying face down. On the floor was a small prescription bottle. It was empty.

I shook him. He woke only slightly and was incoherent. I looked at the label on the pill bottle. Valium, 10 mg. He must have taken the pills before he called me.

I found the phone and dialed 911.

"This is Dr. Mayer." I heard myself say. "I have a medical emergency. Attempted suicide."

I gave them the address and begged them to hurry. Then I tried to keep Ned awake, shaking him gently and talking to him.

The paramedics arrived quickly. They went to work on Ned, put him on a stretcher and took him to the hospital.

The case was out of my hands. I hoped it was only temporary.

Chapter 3

MISJUDGMENTS

I̲T̲ isn't unusual for patients who are depressed, or who sometimes just feel overwhelmed, to ask to be hospitalized. They believe that once they are admitted they will be taken care of or maybe even cured. And, of course, some patients are. But when a patient who I believe is simply looking for a quick fix begins to talk about being committed, I usually suggest that he take a tour of the nearby psychiatric wards. Sometimes the suggestion alone does the trick. If not, a visit to one or two wards, especially if they are in public hospitals, invariably encourages these patients to take more control over their lives, or at least to try.

As a rule, New York City hospitals tend to be crowded and understaffed. Some give you the feeling you have entered the Third World. If I ever need a hospital—and I'm not bleeding to death—my wife has standing instructions to take me to New Jersey. I have learned through experience that it is faster by far to drive the half hour to another state than to try to gain admission to an emergency room in the city, where they are likely to be triaging overdoses, stabbings and assorted other products of urban mayhem.

Ned, however, had no choice. He was in the hands of New York City's Emergency Medical Services, and it simply took him to one of the nearest hospitals. The emergency room staff did their job well. They pumped Ned's stomach, gave him stimulants, probably an amphetamine, to counteract the pills he had swallowed and then admitted him for observation. Ned was lucky. He was alive, with no brain damage.

What came next was more problematic. I believed Ned was suffering from multiple personality disorder, but I also knew that in all probability the hospital staff believed it to be an extremely rare malady. If Ned switched into Terry and started to scream "Don't hurt the baby," the staff would likely misdiagnose his problem as schizophrenia, a more serious illness with an altogether different treatment. Schizophrenia hinders a person's ability to think, to respond emotionally, to remember, to communicate, to interpret reality and to behave appropriately. No one is quite sure what causes it, and the prognosis for a schizophrenic is much worse than for a patient who has multiple personalities. But it isn't hard to see why multiple personality disorder is often mistaken for schizophrenia. Both the schizophrenic and the multiple claim to hear voices, although for the former the voices are imagined and external, while for the latter they come from alter personalities inside of them. As a therapist, I have talked to these internal voices. Indeed, I spend much of my time conversing with them. I have never talked to the voice a schizophrenic hears.

A clinician who has experience with both disorders can discern the difference between schizophrenia and multiplicity, much like doctors who have seen thousands of sore throats can tell before the lab tests come back which ones are strep. Most psychiatric residents, though, lack that experience. When they are in doubt, they often turn to the *Diagnostic and Statistical Manual of Mental Disorders*, which lists symptoms so that a clinician can pick and choose his way to a decision. The trouble is, the manual is written by a committee whose members, while all highly qualified, are also human, and therefore spend hours debating this category versus that before arriving at some kind of compromise. And as soon as an edition is published, there is invariably disagreement and work starts on the next revision.

Anyway, many psychiatric disorders have similar or overlapping symptoms and very often it is hard to find a cubbyhole in which a patient can be placed. Indeed, even though multiple personality disorder now appears under its own heading in the manual, a Canadian colleague of mine, Dr. Colin Ross, in his fine textbook on multiple personality disorder, notes that it is not unusual for a multiple to meet the manual's criteria for 10 different disorders at the same time, including borderline personality, depression, substance abuse, eating disorders, somatization disorder and panic disorder.

I was trained by professors who believed that diagnostic categories largely served the needs of hospital administrators and practitioners who were either insecure or needed to complete insurance forms. Milton Erickson did not even think in terms of disorders. He believed that people go through developmental stages and sometimes get stuck in one of them. It is the therapist's job to get them unstuck. "Your patient has a problem," he would say. "Help him solve it."

One of my supervisors in analytic school put it slightly differently. "Everybody is everything," he said. "Treat the person."

The price of a mistaken diagnosis can be disastrously high. Schizophrenia is treated medically as well as psychotherapeutically, with strong antipsychotic drugs such as Thorazine and Stelazine, which tend to stop hallucinations. Multiple personality disorder, in contrast, is treated with talk, in psychotherapeutic sessions designed to help patients remember events so painful they have been forgotten.

As they finally face this pain, their need for separate alter personalities is eliminated and these alters can be merged into the patient's main personality. Medication generally does not help people with multiple personality disorder. In fact, it can be dangerous.

According to Dr. Frank W. Putnam of the National Institute of Mental Health, 46 percent of clinicians in a survey observed that different personalities of the same patient had varying sensitivities to the same medication. I saw this in a patient I once treated who was taking pain medicine. Sometimes a very small dose would put her to sleep, but other times massive doses of the drug would have no effect. It all depended on which personality took it. I had another patient who was addicted to heroin. When he went through rehabilitation, some of his personalities suffered withdrawal but some did not. And I have heard of cases where one personality takes a pill, then another personality assumes control of the body and takes another kind of pill that causes a bad reaction with the first.

As a result of all this, patients with multiple personality disorder tend to have trouble in hospitals where staff members are not experienced with their illness. Years ago, a multiple I was treating went into a hospital, was diagnosed as a schizophrenic and loaded up with Thorazine, which quickly turned her into a zombie. By the time they stopped giving her the drug, she was so angry about her mistreatment that she became enraged. The hospital staff responded by giving her more drugs and putting her in a locked room. When they finally let her out, she threw another fit, switching into a particularly hostile personality who threatened staff members and even their families. Her doctors, believing they now had proof she was schizophrenic, gave her a series of electric shock treatments. When she continued to get worse, they put her in restraints.

Finally, they allowed me to come to the hospital and try to work with her. Some part of her recognized me as someone who was on her side. At our first session, she switched into a calm, rational alter who, at my suggestion, remained in control for three tranquil days. That was long enough for the hospital to judge that she was better and release her. I suspected they simply wanted nothing more to do with her. And, of course, they believed their treatment was responsible for her recovery, not mine.

I needed to talk with the psychiatrist in charge of Ned's case to make certain he would not be similarly mistreated. But first I had to find him. I tried to phone the hospital to get his name, but the main information line was always busy. I had my electronic phone redial the number every few seconds, but I guess everyone else was doing the same thing.

When I finally got through, the hospital had an automatic answering system that required callers to know the extension of the doctor they were trying to reach, which was of course the very information I was seeking. I finally stayed on the line long enough to get a human, who announced the name of the hospital and then asked me to "please hold." After several minutes, I heard a dial tone, indicating that I had been cut off. After several more tries, I finally got the operator back and practically yelled into the mouthpiece, "This is Dr. Mayer. This is an emergency. Do not put me on hold. Do not put me on hold."

That worked. The operator connected me to one of the hospital's many inpatient psychiatric wards. Then I was switched to another. And another. Finally, I was connected with 8 North, which was Ned's ward. I was told the name of the doctor in charge of his case but, of course, he was not in his office, nor could he be reached. I left my number.

After three days of telephone tag, I finally reached Ned's doctor, an Indian who spoke crisp, British colonial English. I'm certain it was frustration that led me to envision him as Ben Kingsley playing Gandhi. I tried to tell him as politely as possible that this was a possible case of multiple personality disorder. He replied, as I feared and knew he would, that multiple personality disorder was very rare and that most likely Ned was suffering from schizophrenia. He told me Ned had regained consciousness after his suicide attempt but was having audio hallucinations, as if that would convince me of the correctness of his diagnosis. Indeed, Ned was even speaking in strange voices, the doctor said.

I tried to give him the short version of the lecture I often give on multiple personality disorder. I told him that although only 200 cases of the illness were reported in all psychiatric literature up to 1980, there had been more than 2,000 cases documented since then, the result of an increasing sensitivity and sophistication about the disorder. And I believe even this figure to be wildly low. I rattled off the names of the many respected psychiatrists who have given workshops and presentations on multiple personality disorder at annual meetings of the American Psychiatric Association. I offered to come to the hospital and talk to his staff. Ned could serve as a demonstration patient, I suggested.

The doctor patronized me, but I persisted. You can't talk with the voices a schizophrenic hears, I argued, but you can have a conversation with a multiple's voices. Perhaps this was an error, for in retrospect I realize that I lost the battle at this point. The doctor listened with what I could sense was a growing disinterest, if not disrespect, then told me in clipped English essentially to stay off his turf and leave the treatment of hospital patients to the hospital staff. Oh yes, I could visit Ned if I wanted, he said, making it clear our conversation was over.

While riding the subway to the hospital the next day, I tried to focus on what little I knew of Ned's inner world. I wished there had been more time to meet his alter personalities. Treating a multiple is like watching a drama unfold, and it helps to know the cast of characters. Some are friendly; some are hostile. Some are cooperative; some are obstructionist. Some are well-adjusted; some are suicidal. In many multiples, one personality is in charge of the

... "switching" mechanism that determines who is in control of the body at a particular time. Sometimes only a single personality knows the patient's whole history.

I also try to determine whether there is an especially violent alter who may want to avenge the abuse that led to his creation. Psychotherapy can create transference, which is when feelings a patient has for others—usually parents but also siblings and spouses—are focused toward the analyst. In an extreme case of transference, a patient might see the therapist as behaving exactly like a father and may even believe the therapist is going to hurt him, as the father did. That could provoke a violent reaction.

But one of the advantages of working with multiples is the chance to enlist a personality in the therapeutic cause, kind of like an undercover agent. After all, much of the work of therapy goes on when the patient is at home, between sessions. An older alter can take care of a younger one, in effect helping to raise them as an older brother or sister might raise a younger sibling. Beth, Toby's five-year-old alter, would kick and scream whenever I went on vacation. But Toby also had an adult alter named Anna who would read stories to Beth to calm her.

I remember treating several multiples who, after particularly emotional sessions, would be so distraught that they could not find their way home. Sometimes they would wander all over the city, getting lost and switching rapidly in and out of different personalities, which made getting or remembering directions virtually impossible. So before a session I anticipated would be rough I would find a relatively unemotional alter and instruct him to gather the personalities who were likely to become upset in a separate room—an imaginary room inside the patient's head, of course. That way, they would not hear anything that went on. The calm alter would also be assigned to take the patient home.

As I headed for the hospital I hoped that I might be able to talk to Ned and perhaps get him to switch to a more cooperative alter for a few days. I picked up the pass in the lobby and took the elevator to the eighth floor. At the far end of the narrow hall was a pair of locked doors. A uniformed guard was seated in front. I showed him my pass. He checked a list, picked up the phone and told the person on the other end that I was here.

After a few moments, Ned's doctor came through the doors. I had been correct; he was a young Indian resident, tall and thin, wearing a white hospital coat with an identification badge pinned to his left breast pocket. With a wave of his hand, he motioned me into his office, to the left of the doors. It had just room enough for an institutional metal desk and two metal chairs, one that swiveled, which was for him, and a stationary one for me.

After exchanging pleasantries the doctor told me that he found Ned's case unusual and disturbing. When Ned recovered from the overdose he seemed to be doing better, but then he began having psychotic episodes in which he would scream something about a baby or a murder. The doctor wasn't sure what it meant. And sometimes, he said, Ned would act like a child, flailing his arms about wildly and stamping his feet. There had been another episode earlier in the day and Ned had to be heavily sedated. He was secluded in what they called a "quiet room." The doctor apologized for not contacting me and saving me the trip, since it was doubtful Ned would respond to me. I told him I wanted to see Ned anyway. He nodded.

After unlocking the doors, the doctor walked me through the dayroom, which could have been a set for *The Snake Pit*. The floor was covered with worn linoleum tiles in a black-and-white checkerboard. On one side, a dozen metal chairs were clustered around two long tables. Across from them a pair of battered sofas faced each other. There were about 20 patients. Some were staring at a television set that was blaring a quiz show; some were playing cards, and some were just wandering about. Most wore green hospital gowns under bathrobes. A few had on street clothes. The air was rank with cigarette smoke.

We went down another hall with a series of doors on one side, each with a little window. The doctor stopped at one of them and pointed. I looked through the window into a tiny, cell-like chamber, with padding on the floor and walls. On the ceiling was a single, dim light bulb covered by a wire grill. Ned was lying in the center of the floor, in a fetal position. I couldn't see his face clearly. His sandy hair was matted with sweat.

Ned's doctor was right. There was no point in trying to talk to him.

WHEN I phoned a few days later I received even more disturbing news. The doctor told me that Ned had come out of the quiet room and had started to improve. They had even allowed him to take phone calls from his parents, who were very concerned and had sent him some flowers. But then without warning he had made a suicide attempt in the hospital, trying to cut his wrists with the top of a metal soda can. He was now under a 24-hour-a-day watch.

Two days later Ned's doctor called to tell me that Ned was better and that I could see him. When I got to the hospital, Ned was in the day room, dressed in a tattered but clean gown and sitting at one of the tables with three other patients, staring into space. He seemed to know who I was, but I had difficulty keeping his attention.

I tried to get Ned to switch into another alter, but the drugs he had been given were too powerful for me to overcome. I stayed a little while, decided that it was futile and went home. I called some friends at a hospital in Philadelphia and explored the possibility of a transfer. They agreed to take Ned, but there was a serious obstacle—his insurance did not cover out-of-state psychiatric units, only hospitals in New York. So he was stuck.

Two days later I visited Ned again. When I got to the locked doors I was told that he was back in isolation. I couldn't find his doctor, but another resident said Ned had again become violent. He wanted to wear his jeans and T-shirt, not a hospital gown, and threw a fit when he was told he couldn't. I suggested that maybe Ned felt dehumanized by the gown and that normal clothes might make him feel more like a normal person. The resident replied that there were rules and Ned had to follow them. The hospital ran on a behavior modification system, and patients had to wear gowns until they earned the right to wear clothes.

I went home wondering how I had gotten into such a mess with a patient who, until recently, was showing signs of progress. After all, while he was seeing me he had started medical school. I was Ned's therapist, the person who knew him best, and yet I had no power to change anything now. The hospital was in charge. No one would listen to me.

I resolved to give it one more try. I got the name of Ned's doctor's supervisor and after several more calls reached him. Maybe that was a good omen, I remember thinking as I began. I told him that I was Ned's therapist and gave him some background on the case. I said I suspected Ned had multiple personality disorder and that the drugs he was being given were contraindicated. In fact, the hospital's entire treatment plan was making Ned worse. I pleaded with him to stop the drugs, let Ned wear his own clothes and let me work with him. I was sure I could get him to follow the hospital's rules.

But the supervisor was unbending. Since I was not on the hospital staff, I could not work with Ned. Then he explained, in an even more condescending manner than Ned's doctor, the hospital's rationale for Ned's treatment. They should change the name of the hospital to the Franz Kafka Medical Center, I remember thinking to myself as he droned on. Ned might be locked away for years. They would medicate him into a stupor so that he would be easy to control, and if necessary, keep him in the padded room. Complaining would only lead to more sedation. Since Ned had been admitted after a suicide attempt, he could not be released until the psychiatric staff ruled that he would not harm himself or others. Yes, he was stuck.

As I was listening to the supervisor, I thought of a story a colleague once told me. A babbling man dressed in a white sheet was picked up and hospitalized. He kept trying to get out and couldn't. Then he made a phone call and 20 babbling people dressed in sheets showed up. It turned out they were all members of a religious group that dressed in sheets and babbled. So the hospital let him out.

PERHAPS Ned found a way not to take the drugs. Perhaps he figured out the hospital's system. In any event, a week or so after my conversation with the supervisor Ned himself called me from the pay phone in the hall near the dayroom. He told me that he was feeling better and wanted to get out of the hospital. I told him to simply behave himself for a little while longer and I might be able to get him released. He said he would try, and he succeeded. Ten days later he was back in his apartment.

But Ned was hardly in good shape after his ordeal. He was unable to go to school and spent most of his time just sitting around, watching a digital clock tick off the minutes. He continued to see me, but for the first few weeks after the hospitalization therapy was not productive. Ned was depressed. Memories of killing a baby in some sort of satanic ritual were haunting him, making him feel confused and guilty.

I tried to get him to talk about the ritual, but he refused, saying he didn't remember it. He also did not want to be hypnotized. He was obviously frightened of summoning up any more memories.

I worked hard to alleviate his guilt, telling him that if indeed the scene he remembered was real it was not his fault. Someone else's hand had gone around his and murdered the child. And he was only a child himself. What could he have done in a room filled with all those adults?

This made sense to him, and in time his depression seemed to lift and he started to get a little life back in him. I was further relieved when he told me that his parents were sending him cards and wanted him to come home to recuperate, although he didn't seem to want much to do with them.

Then one day, without warning, I got a call from a friend of Ned's telling me that Ned had jumped in front of a subway train. Ned was dead.

I was shocked. His spirits had seemed better. I was sure we were turning the corner. Clearly, I'd been wrong. I thought about the case, trying to make sense out of it. I could only conclude that Ned had wanted to kill himself all along. He tried to do it at home and failed. He tried again in the hospital and was prevented. Then he got out of the hospital and succeeded. Still, I wondered what drove him to do it and if I'd missed some subtle clue. Was it the shame of having more than one personality inside of him? The guilt of believing he had killed another person? Or maybe it was something we had not yet uncovered?

I called Ned's doctor at the hospital and told him the news. He suggested that we discuss the case and we met that evening. He was kind to me, telling me I should not feel responsible. When they let Ned out of the hospital, he said, the staff felt that the crisis was over. He then told me something that I had heard many times before but needed to hear again: if someone wants to kill himself, he will, and no one can stop him.

To prove his point, he told me about people in the various hospitals in which he had worked who made attempt after attempt. Some were very creative in their efforts at self-destruction. One patient broke a light bulb and used the glass to cut his wrist. Another wove a rope out of dental floss and tried to hang herself. Sometimes patients even managed to kill themselves while under 24-hour watch. If a hospital could not prevent suicide, what could an analyst in private practice do? We talked for a long time about the hazards of the profession. I thanked him and took my leave.

On the train home I wondered whether the motorman saw Ned or felt the impact. I thought of the nameless people who had to clean up the tracks. What must they have thought? I thought about mistakes I might have made in Ned's therapy. I ran the case over and over in my mind. What did I miss?

Chapter 4

REBECCA

My office is about 12 feet wide by 20 feet long, with a high, plaster-beamed ceiling typical of what the real-estate ads refer to as a pre-war apartment building. The room is painted light mauve.

I sit in a reclining chair in the far corner, across from the door. Behind me is a tall bookcase and a teak desk with a phone, an answering machine, a computer and a printer. Perched on the air conditioner in the window over the desk sit four teddy bears, one of which is named Jasper, and a stuffed chimp named Max, gifts from colleagues and patients. I use them from time to time with child-abuse victims, sometimes as props to help them re-enact incidents they cannot talk about on their own, sometimes merely for soothing, as I tried to do with Ned. Concerned about how this little menagerie looked to other patients, I have often chided myself for not putting them out of sight.

Along the wall next to the desk is my analytic couch, which is covered in camel-colored vinyl. On the wall behind the couch are diplomas and certificates I have earned over

58

years of study. I hung them there early in my career as a substitute for experience, and like the stuffed animals they have remained.

Opposite the couch is a bentwood swivel chair for patients who wish to sit facing me rather than recline. On that wall are two large Kabuki prints by the artist Al Hirschfeld. One is of a snarly samurai dressed in a black robe and holding a red and tan umbrella. In the other, a demure Japanese woman wears a traditional dress and an apologetic expression. Long after I bought the drawings I learned that Kabuki actors were always male.

The rule at my analytic school was that every patient should use the couch. Failure to do so was considered a sign of psychological resistance. That Freud used a couch would probably have been enough of an endorsement all by itself, but there are sound therapeutic reasons for employing one. A patient who lies on a couch is unable to see the analyst and can not pick up visual cues that might influence what he says or thinks or feels. All of us react consciously and unconsciously to others. Some people do it to a fault, creating what my colleagues call "false selves." A few carry it so far that they become Zelig-like reflections of whomever they are with. But the couch enables a patient to explore his true self with a minimum of external influence.

I generally encourage patients to use the couch, but most of the time it does little good even to suggest it to those who have been victims of child abuse, at least in the beginning. These are highly traumatized patients and they simply cannot abide having the therapist out of their sight. Their reservoir of trust is so low they must see him at all times.

The door to my office is directly behind the patient's chair. Some abuse victims like this arrangement, apparently figuring that they can get out of the room quickly should the need arise. Others hate having a door behind them. Like Wyatt Earp, they like to sit with their back to the wall, preferably in a corner.

As a rule, abuse victims are so exquisitely sensitive to

their environment that they notice even tiny changes, especially, it seems, in their therapists' offices. If I look at a book and put it back in a different spot on the shelf, I can count on one of them spotting it the next day. Their radar senses that something is different, that there is cause for alarm. Sometimes they will mention it, which is probably an unconscious way of reminding me that they are constantly on the alert, always watching. These patients are like skittish squirrels that scamper up trees whenever anyone approaches. Once, on an uncomfortably warm and sticky day, I got up on the spur of the moment to take off a sweater and my patient shot out of her chair, heading for the door. I have since learned not to make sudden movements.

I can understand the intensity of their fears. Growing up in an abusive world, they *had* to be constantly on guard. Pain could be inflicted at any moment, for any reason. Toby used to tell me that she would know trouble was coming when she saw a certain look in her mother's eyes. Years later, she is still fearful. The past is the present and the future. The environment is still potentially hostile. No place is safe. No one can be trusted. It is a horrible way to live, I thought to myself as I waited for Rebecca to arrive for our first consultation.

SHE came to me for the reason many patients now come to me: She had told her previous analyst that she believed there were other people living inside her, and he didn't believe her.

He was a classical analyst who said very little during their sessions. This approach can make patients anxious. Sometimes they will respond by trying to manipulate their therapist into a reaction, much like a baby cries when it wants to be held. That's what Rebecca's analyst believed she was doing, feigning multiplicity to get him to give her more attention.

"You're just inventing these characters," he told her.

They argued about this for two years. Therapy became a battle. It was like a scene from one of those wildlife documentaries on television, in which two rams go at it. They eye each other, lower their heads and run ahead at full steam. They hit with a jolt, horn against horn, stumble, shake out the cobwebs, rear on their hind legs and butt each other again and again.

Finally, Rebecca decided it was time to stop fighting and seek another opinion.

She arrived precisely on time, extending her hand assertively to shake mine. But I noticed that she made sure there was plenty of room between us as she entered my apartment, walked into the office and sat down in the bentwood chair. As I closed the door and moved around her to my chair, I could feel the vigilance in her glance. Only when I had settled in my chair did she seem to relax.

She was tiny—five feet tall and probably less than a hundred pounds. Her red, shoulder-length hair was parted in the center and tucked behind her ears. Whenever she shook her head, strands would slip out and cover her eyes, and she would automatically tuck them back again.

Her eyes were small, round and deeply set in dark sockets, making her look older than her 25 years. She wore no makeup, no nail polish and, I noted gratefully, no perfume. (After a full day of therapy my office sometimes smells like the cosmetics section of a department store.) But she more than compensated with jewelry. Around her neck hung an amber stone, a Jewish star and three other gold chains that brought the necklace count to five. She wore a ring on every finger of each hand, including her thumbs, which made her slender fingers look as though they were wired together. Around her wrists were innumerable plastic bracelets of various thicknesses and hues that clanged whenever Rebecca moved her arms. The jewelry struck me as interesting, since most patients in the midst of therapy dress drably. Their appearance usually brightens as they make progress.

Rebecca told me that she was born and raised in an upper-middle-class Long Island town. Her father was a successful attorney who specialized in immigration matters and international adoptions. Her mother dabbled in oils and sculpture in a small studio attached to their house. Rebecca had two younger sisters, but told me she had not had any contact with them for quite a while.

She went to private schools and then one of the "seven sister" colleges. After graduation she moved to New York City and set out to earn a master's degree in criminal justice. It was an unusual choice, but then she was a lawyer's daughter.

She began therapy while in college with a pair of complaints common to young women—anorexia and bulimia, two eating disorders. An anorexic thinks she is too fat and compulsively diets; a bulimic binges on food and then sometimes forces herself to regurgitate immediately afterward. These disorders seem to be prevalent among patients who were sexually abused, I suspect because their weight may be the only thing these victims feel they can control, and they can use it to make themselves look less attractive.

Rebecca changed therapists a few times before finding one with whom she thought she could work. And for a while her therapy went well. The bulimia and the anorexia receded. Her weight stayed constant.

Then came her first set of graduate-school exams. She was barreling through a criminal psychology test when she suddenly felt a wave of anxiety. She became more and more agitated. Finally, she had to put down her pen and leave the classroom. Unable to go back to school, she dropped out and soon was working as an office temporary.

As Rebecca told her psychiatrist about her experience during the exam, she had a faint but unmistakable recollection that something terrible had occurred in her past. Over the next few days and weeks, she had dreams and pieces of dreams that filled in some of the details, bit by bit. Then, a few therapy sessions later, she was able to put it all together: she was sure she had been raped as a child. She remembered seeing a man standing in the hallway, looking at her as she lay in her bed. He came closer. She screamed out. The next image she recalled was of a man raping her. When it was over, she looked at his face and saw it was her father.

That memory was a watershed. Soon, Rebecca was having flashbacks of other childhood rapes and episodes of abuse. Sometimes these incidents were related by a "child" who lived within her. Other times, she would find letters around her house describing abusive scenes or telling her about other people living inside her.

She told her doctor about all this. She showed him the letters and even brought some of the people forth to meet him during her sessions. But her analyst just sat there and accused her of making it all up. He told Rebecca that her anxiety all stemmed from the death of her father, which had occurred a few weeks before the eventful exam. He said she was just inventing reasons not to face her real problem, which was her unconscious desire to have sex with her father.

The more Rebecca insisted that she had other people inside of her, the more her doctor insisted that she didn't. I could understand his position, given his feelings about multiple personality disorder. But couldn't he see that his approach to therapy wasn't working this time? That Rebecca was getting worse? He was behaving like the mythical Procrustes, who only had one size of bed in his inn. If a lodger was too tall, he would simply cut off enough of him to fit.

I don't believe a therapist should ever oppose a patient or force his theoretical beliefs on one. It serves no purpose, except to make her plant her feet and argue more strongly. Even if you convince a patient that she is wrong, she will rarely stay convinced. Usually she will just back down for the moment and then go back to her original belief, to which is now added resentment.

Desperate for confirmation and support, and frustrated by her doctor, Rebecca started attending meetings of Survivors of Incest Anonymous, a 12-step, self-help program modeled on Alcoholics Anonymous. At one meeting, she met a woman who was in therapy with someone who had heard me speak at a conference. This woman, who also suffered from multiple personality disorder, suggested that Rebecca seek out a therapist familiar with the problem. That brought her to me.

"THESE people who you say are inside you. Can you talk to them?" I asked Rebecca.

"Some of them," she said. Her bracelets jangled as she shifted in her chair.

"Only some?"

"My Board of Directors has not let me meet them all, because I can't handle it yet. That's what they tell me."

"Board of Directors?"

"My system is highly organized. The Board of Directors runs everything. It has a Chairman, who will not talk to anyone. There is a guide to lead everyone through the system."

"Sounds complicated."

"Yes. It has to be highly organized because of the number of alters."

"How many are there?"

"Over four hundred at last count," she said, fidgeting with one of her rings. "And we are constantly finding more."

I was starting to understand why her last analyst felt the way he did. More than 400 alters. I had never heard of such a thing. Researchers in the field were writing about the increase in the number of personalities that multiple personality patients were reporting, and the current average was up to a few dozen. But 400? I was stunned and more than a little skeptical. However, I didn't have time to pursue this with her, because she cut my thoughts off.

"And there are Gatekeepers."

"What do they do?" I said, preferring to talk about something concrete, rather than her overcrowded internal world.

"They decide what I remember. They protect me. They were the ones who kept all of this away from me, until I was taking that psych test."

"Why do you think they let you know about your father then?" I asked.

"Because they wanted me to fail, so I wouldn't become a criminologist."

She paused, looked at her watch and began to play with the clasp. Then she raised her eyes to meet mine.

"Because my family was involved in some strange activities."

"Strange activities?" I repeated calmly.

"I don't know whether I can tell you. I'll have to find out."

Rebecca closed her eyes. Her head drooped onto her right shoulder, then rose with a jolt. Her shoulders stiffened. When she opened her eyes they had a fearful look, darting around the room, inspecting everything in the office.

"Who are you?" I asked, aware from my experience with other multiples that she had switched personalities.

"The Detective."

It was a woman's voice, but there was something masculine about it.

"My job is to determine if the situation is safe. You never know where they might be."

With that, the body before me slumped. The eyes closed and the head tilted to the side. Then it straightened. I suspected that Rebecca was back.

"The Board says I can tell you the story," she said, opening her eyes. My family was involved with a group of people who would meet and dress up. In robes. And they wore masks to cover their faces, animal masks."

She hesitated a moment, uncertain whether to go on.

"They chanted these songs. And said prayers, strange prayers. They were, well, they prayed to the devil. They believed in him."

She continued quietly, now fingering her bracelets. "They told me I would be a high priestess. But I left them and now I'm sure that they are tracking me and at some point will find me and try to get me back. I know too much about them."

"Can you tell me about them?"

"Are you sure you want to know?" she said. There was an edge to her voice, almost an eerie quality. "It could be dangerous for you."

I told her I wasn't frightened. Perhaps I should have been, but I just couldn't take what she was telling me seriously.

"They have meetings. They read from ancient texts. They chant ancient incantations. They sacrifice animals and sometimes even children. Then they eat the hearts and drink the blood. They believe that Satan requires this."

She paused and tucked a thick strand of red hair behind her right ear.

"They keep women hidden on farms. Breeders, they call them. The breeders produce the children. But they also import children for their sacrifices from other countries. They have a network. That's why I wear this."

She held up the piece of amber that hung around her neck.

"To ward off evil. To protect me. From them."

She paused and looked at me. She was utterly calm, almost emotionless, despite what she was saying.

"And that's why I converted to Judaism. All religions have the problem of explaining how a god can allow evil things to occur. Jews believe that man was given free will and can exercise that free will in the service of good or evil. Christians believe that there is a separate entity for evil that is in a struggle with God. Judaism made the most sense to me. Also, Judaism does not make a person into a god, or make a god into a person. And I needed its rituals, to replace the horrible rituals. I have experimented with all the major religions—studied their doctrines, attended their services, spent time at ashrams and monasteries. Judaism was the only one that I could relate to. Until these memories came up, I never knew why. Now I guess I do."

Smart, I thought to myself.

"So, Rebecca, why do you need me, if you know all this by yourself?"

"Something happened to me at that exam, and since then I have been having these memories. Every night I would remember something else. Another grotesque ceremony. Another personality inside me. And I know there is much more. But I'm not sure how much is true. I need someone who has experience with all of this. I want you to tell me whether or not this is real, and what I should do about it."

Those were questions I couldn't answer, not right now anyway, and perhaps not ever. But it seemed clear to me that Rebecca was a multiple. I had met one internal personality, the Detective. As for her Board of Directors, multiples very often have what is called an "inner self-helper," some all-knowing part that analysts often enlist to help uncover repressed memories. I was hoping this Board might be similarly helpful. Perhaps I would meet the Chairman, who I suspected might be the highest in a hierarchy of self-helpers, and thus the most valuable.

But the satanism was another matter. Some of the episodes Rebecca talked about were eerily reminiscent of Ned's haunting memory. What were the odds of encountering two patients with such similar accounts of ritual abuse? How could these stories be true? Baby killings. Breeders. Goblets of blood. Robed figures dancing wildly and chanting their homage to Satan. Do such things really exist?

I decided to accept Rebecca as a patient and we negotiated times for our sessions and agreed on a fee.

If I could find a way to help her, I thought as I watched her walk down the hall from my office, I might somehow learn what happened to Ned.

Chapter 5

THE CEREMONY

"I feel understood, at last," Rebecca told me as we began our second session. "It's different from my other therapy. You're different."

But after this promising—and flattering—start to our next therapy session, things soon grew more troubling. Rebecca told me she was having nightmares, vivid, horrifying dreams that caused enough anxiety to break through the sleep barrier and keep her up all night.

Patients often will start to dream—or more precisely, since sleep researchers tell us we all dream every night, start to remember their dreams—when they begin to take therapy earnestly. It is terrible to wake up from a nightmare, of course, but it is good for therapy. It means memories are coming to the surface.

Rebecca was silent now. I monitored my thoughts and

feelings, as I always do while working with a patient. Freud said that the analyst's mind must be in three places at once—listening to his patient, listening to himself and keeping track of the interaction between analyst and patient. A therapist's thoughts and feelings are supposed to be influenced by the patient's thoughts and feelings. Ideally, patient and therapist should be like two tuning forks with the same frequency: when one is struck, the other starts to vibrate.

I was feeling anxious. Was Rebecca also feeling anxious? I wasn't sure. This was only our second session, and I hardly knew her. I decided I would wait a moment to see what would happen. Let her take the lead, my instincts told me.

The silence continued. And continued. And continued. As I sat there, I began to see Rebecca's expression and posture start to change. It was almost imperceptible at first. She lowered her head. Then she turned, so that she was looking at the wall with the Hirschfelds. She scrunched up her facial muscles. She squinted her eyes. And then, without warning, she bounded out of her chair and started to pace back and forth in the center of the room.

"I can't sleep," she said, trembling.

Her voice somehow seemed like that of a younger person, perhaps a pre-adolescent girl.

"It's going to happen again. She's coming in. I can hear her. She's getting closer. I have to get out, I have to run. Where? Out the door. No, she's in the hall. The window. That's it. But she'll catch me. Run, run. Run, run. Help me. Somebody help me."

Who was this? I thought to myself. Certainly not the Detective. What prompted the switch? It happened so quickly, with no more provocation than a few moment's silence.

"Who are you?" I said, attempting to make contact.

"Arlene."

She paused. Her eyes were darting all around my office.

"I'm frightened. I hear her coming to get me. It always happens. I can't sleep. I watch the clock all night, waiting for it to get light outside. Time goes so slowly. Some nights nothing happens. But sometimes she comes in to get me. Tonight she is coming. I can hear her. She is coming."

"What happens when she comes?"

"I don't know. She comes in and the next thing I remember, it's night again and I'm here watching the clock, waiting for morning, hoping she won't come in."

Even before I could begin to think about what she was saying, Rebecca's head began dipping to the left and the right. Now her eyes just stared ahead vacantly.

"Yes, Momma, I'm coming. I'm getting dressed."

The change in her tone told me she had switched again. By now, she was back in the bentwood chair.

"Who are you?"

"I am Obedience, and today I am twelve years old."

"What do you mean, twelve years old?"

"I can be different ages at different times."

Internal personalities are "born" at the time of a painful incident. Sometimes they remain frozen at that age. Sometimes they grow older, usually as they absorb more abuse. But I had never come across an internal personality who could be different ages at different times. Perhaps this personality was formed in response to an event that was repeated over and over again. I didn't really have time to think too much about it, though. I decided to turn off my cognitive mind and simply react to my patient. I hoped Freud would understand.

"Tell me what you do."

"Whatever Momma says. That other one is too frightened. I live inside of her."

"Inside of Rebecca?"

"Inside of Arlene. I come out when Momma comes. I can't leave Arlene here. She might run away. I know that if we run, we will get killed. I know better. We have to do whatever Momma says or terrible things will happen to us."

Apparently she was a multiple within a multiple. A riddle within an enigma. I decided to keep the dialogue going, making a mental note to try to come back later to the "terrible things."

"What happens next?"

"I get dressed. Momma and I get in the car. We drive to that place. Nobody talks. I sit very still. I have to be a good girl . . . good girl. It is very important. Quiet . . . quiet. Still . . . still."

She paused between repetitions.

"What place?" I said, just trying to keep her talking.

"A farmhouse. On a back road, way out in the woods. It takes a long time to get there. We've been there many times.

"There are other cars parked outside. Momma tells me to go into a little room and get undressed. I take off all my clothes, like I always do, and sit on the floor." Keeping her eyes lowered, she folded her ringed fingers in her lap.

"Then what?"

"One of the devils comes in to get me. Yes. Wearing a black robe. He has horns coming out of his head. He takes my hand and leads me into the other room. The big room. All the others are there."

"What happens next?"

"It's a big room. There are candles all around. The candles are black. They are dancing in a circle, around a table in the center of the room. They are all chanting words, but I don't understand them. They chant and dance, faster and faster. I am in the center of the circle. I am naked."

Her body shuddered weakly, almost imperceptibly. She was now standing in front of me and although she was fully dressed she had put her small hands over her breasts and pubic area, as if to cover her nakedness.

"I am scared. I have to get out . . . out. Run . . . run. Get away. No . . . no."

Just when I thought she was going to scream, she became calm. Staring straight ahead, she continued the story, but in a voice that spoke more slowly and sounded older. Another personality? Perhaps the episode she was recalling was broken up into sections, and each part was invested in a different alter.

"The devil reaches to the table, between two candles, and picks up a silver cup. He holds it up for the others to see. Then he comes over and pours it over my head."

She stopped for a moment, frantically wiping her hair with her hands.

"Ich. Ich. Blood."

Once again, the changed modulation of her voice told me there had been a switch to another personality.

"I have to get out. No, where can I go? They're all around me. Help me. Help me.

"I must not run. They will kill me."

I had treated many multiples, probably more than 20, but I had never seen one switch so many times in so short a period. It was like watching dancers under strobe lights at a discotheque. I had no time to think about the functions or roles of all these personalities. All I knew was that they helped Rebecca resolve the dilemma of being frightened and wanting to run away from the devils, but at the same time being afraid that she would be killed if she was caught. But was any of this terrible scene real? Or was it just the imagination of a troubled patient? There was nothing for me to do but let her continue. It was obvious I was no longer in control of the session.

"The head devil motions to another devil, who brings him a knife. The big one holds it over his head and says, 'Hail Satan.' The others begin to shout with him.

"He comes closer. He puts the knife in my hand, picks up the goblet and pours blood over it.

"Another devil brings in a baby. It is crying. He places it on the table and pours blood on its chest. They all look at me.

"The child's eyes are open, staring at me. I feel nauseous.

I am going to throw up. Maybe I should drop the knife. Maybe I should kill the devil. No, there are too many of them."

Another shudder. Another switch. I sensed immediately that this new personality had a much stronger presence than the others. I felt a bit intimidated, like when I was a child and went to temple on an important holy day.

"My name is Artonoxima."

She spoke deliberately, in a commanding monotone.

"I am a priestess initiate. It is my job to kill the baby. I must do it well, so that I can get my robe and move on to the next step in my training. I must do Satan's work."

At this point Rebecca raised both hands over her head as if she were holding a knife, ready to strike. Her bracelets slipped down her arms. I could not believe what I was seeing.

"We offer this child to Satan, our master," she said. "Hail Satan. May he accept our offering."

She made a plunging motion into the rainbow colored pillow at the head of my analytic couch. She did it again. Then she made some sawing motions on the pillow before putting the imaginary knife down. She reached out with her right hand as if she was grabbing something, then held her hand over her head.

"This is the heart. This is the essence. We will now partake of the offering."

She made some motions that reminded me of someone carving a roast and serving it to dinner guests. What was she doing now? Could she be putting a piece in her mouth? The thought repulsed me. Was that what this ghastly pantomime was about?

Artonoxima showed no emotion. She was cold and clinical. In contrast, there was a tightening in my throat that made it hard to swallow. I thought of the time I tried to eat fried beetles, which are to Calcutta what pretzels are to Philadelphia. They crunched.

"Each devil takes a piece of the heart," Artonoxima

continued. "They all hold it up and shout, 'Hail Satan,' and then they eat it. They dance around me, chanting. They go faster and faster. I am the center, the center of their attention. They are honoring me. They are exalting me. I did my job well. I will get my robe."

She went through the motions of putting on an imaginary robe, looking smug, her necklaces jangling as she moved. Then she shuddered, and I sensed she was gone.

Whatever personality took over next went straight to my couch and lay down. Putting her arms over her head and spreading her legs slightly apart, the tiny woman before me started to groan. She spread her legs wider and wider. More groaning. It was unmistakably sexual.

"They are holding me down. They are all rubbing oil over me. On my chest. Even on my legs."

Her frail body started to undulate. After a few minutes she relaxed. Then she started again. She did this over and over again. So many times I lost count. Finally, she stopped. She just lay there, exhausted, arms at her sides. I was certain she had acted out a series of rapes, although whether she had actually endured them or not I could not know.

Just when I thought she was finished, Rebecca began to scream. I looked at her eyes. They seemed like tiny pieces of coal. She screamed again and again. Her mouth got wider and wider.

I sat like a stone, not feeling anything, trying to make my mind think. The woman before me had re-enacted murder, cannibalism and rape. But I found myself worrying about whether anyone was hearing her screams. The walls of my office are solid plaster and brick, I thought. I remembered that the room above me had been the playroom for children who had long since grown up and gone off to school. It was probably empty now. As is customary for therapists, my office is on the first floor. There was nothing under me except the basement, and that was probably empty, too. But what about the sidewalk outside the window? What if someone should walk by, hear Rebecca's screams and call the police? I suppose I was heartened by the fact that this was New York, a city in which people witness all manner of criminal mayhem with hardly a second thought.

Later, reflecting on my thoughts and my apparent lack of feelings for Rebecca, I concluded that my counter-transference machinery had short-circuited. In theory, I should have felt some of her pain, some of her horror, some of her fear. I should have empathized with her. But her story was so brutal and so weird that *I* must have dissociated.

After I don't know how long, Rebecca's screaming stopped. I had no idea which personality was before me.

"They take me into the next room," she said after a while, picking up where she had left off. "The women come in. They lay me on a fur rug on the floor. They then rub my body with oil. My body hurts, but it also feels good. They do it slowly. It feels good."

I sat in my chair and watched her writhe, but more gently now than before. Her body jerked a few times, then relaxed. She looked calm. I realized that she was re-enacting an orgasm. Thank God she couldn't see me. I am sure I looked every bit as astonished as I felt. I had watched patients re-enact rapes, beatings, even murders before. But I never watched a woman re-enact an orgasm in my office, on my analytic couch. True, one of my patients had once tried to seduce me—or maybe just shock me, I'm still not sure—by walking into my office, opening her coat and demonstrating that she was a natural redhead. I simply told her to close her coat, go home and make sure she was properly clothed for her next appointment.

I decided to follow the cardinal rule of psychoanalysis: When in doubt, do nothing. I put on my best empathetic expression, the one that they taught me in shrink school, in case she looked over at me, and waited. It was at times like this that I most appreciated the couch.

Rebecca—or whoever she was now—was sitting up on the couch, starting to talk again.

"I lay there a while," she said calmly, tucking her red hair behind her ears. "There was music playing softly. Someone pulled a blanket over me. There was this smell, some sort of fragrance in the air. I rested a while. Then I was told by one of the women to get dressed and go to the car. I went into the other room. I saw the bathroom door open and went in. There was blood under my nails, so I scrubbed them. I tried to get the oil and blood out of my hair. I scrubbed and scrubbed—I wanted to scrub my skin off. I dried myself with a towel and put my clothes on and went outside to the car. My mother was there, in the driver's seat. I remember she just sat there and said hello, the way she did when she picked me up after school. We drove home and I went to bed."

With that, she got off the couch, walked across the room, sat down again in the bentwood chair and looked at me. She had become the 25-year-old woman who had walked into my office what seemed like days before, except that she looked exhausted. I checked the clock and saw that, amazingly, we still had a few minutes left in the session. I didn't know what to say.

"Are you back?"

"Yes." She was fidgeting with her rings again.

"That was quite an experience. What do you remember of it?"

"All of it, I think. Once it comes up like that, I know what happened. Before it comes up, I have no knowledge of it. But afterward, yes. Sometimes it comes up like that at home. It used to come up like that when I was in therapy before."

"What would your doctor do?"

"He would just sit there, and not say anything. Sometimes when I finished, I noticed that he had turned his swivel chair around. He would tell me that I was hysterical. He would tell me that I should talk about these things rather than acting them out. I would have loved to do that, Dr. Mayer, but I can't. They just happen. I can't control it."

"You have to agree that all this is shocking," I said, a little lamely. "Most people would have difficulty with it."

"Then they shouldn't be therapists," she said angrily.

The phrase, "Physician, heal thyself," came to mind. Fortunately, my own psychiatric structure had held. I was shocked, even repelled, but not paralyzed. I knew that if I wanted to help Rebecca I had to be able to handle whatever she threw my way. I could not afford to take two for flinching.

Because of her experience with her previous therapist, it was essential that I convince Rebecca that I believed her, no matter how bizarre or farfetched her re-enactments seemed. But I also knew that, given the mistrust multiples typically feel, I had to be absolutely honest with her. She would sense anything less.

As she left my office, I wondered how I ever could manage to do both at once.

Chapter 6

DOUBTS

THE unconscious mind just seems to lead us in the right direction doesn't it?

I did not plan to be a psychoanalyst. When I was young I wanted to go to Annapolis and become a naval officer. But my parents were the children of immigrants—my father could not read or write, and my mother did not finish high school. When they were divorced, I went to work part-time to help out. Offered a scholarship to Rutgers College of Pharmacy, I abandoned thoughts of a naval career, hoping instead to emulate three uncles who made good livings as pharmacists.

In 1956 I was licensed to practice pharmacy and within a few years I owned two drugstores. But while I was financially successful, I was intellectually unfulfilled. I found myself taking courses in subjects that my scientific training had left out—philosophy, literature, history, art history, comparative religion, sociology and psychology. In 1962 I sold the stores and used the proceeds to support my family while I went back to Rutgers for a doctorate in history. By the late 1960s, I was an assistant professor at Kean College, in Union, New Jersey.

I enjoyed teaching, but still felt something was missing. I realized I was ignoring an entire dimension of my field. I was teaching my students about economic, political and sociological influences, but not about the psychological aspects of events. Once again I went back to school, this time to become a psychohistorian, someone who is aware of the psychological dimensions of history as well as the history of psychology. I envisioned myself teaching courses in psychobiography, the history of the family, the psychology of warfare and other such subjects.

Since I was not interested in another academic degree, I enrolled in the American Institute for Psychotherapy and Psychoanalysis in New York City. Although it was a training institute for therapists, I remember telling Ross Thalheimer, the director, that I had a more academic end in mind. I took courses with psychiatrists, psychologists and social workers in the evening while I taught at Kean College during the day. I was also analyzed, a requirement of the program. Thinking that I would someday write about the history of the profession, I traveled around the country to study different methods and approaches—Gestalt therapy with Fritz Perls, psychosynthesis training with Harry Sloan, bioenergetics with Alexander Lowen, psychodrama with James Sachs, rational emotive therapy with Albert Ellis, hypnosis with Milton Erickson and family systems theory with Gregory Bateson and Jay Haley.

After my second year at the institute, Dr. Thalheimer called me in. He knew I still had no intention of practicing psychotherapy, but asked me to reconsider. Some of my teachers had told him I would be good at it, he said.

I reminded him of my unorthodox background. He insisted my pharmacological experience and knowledge of history would be assets. And he reminded me that Freud himself had argued that people with varied backgrounds make the best analysts.

After much soul-searching, and at the urging of my training analyst, Heindrich Reutenbeek, I accepted my first patient from the institute's clinic, the Community Guidance Service. I spent a lot of time worrying about how my office should be set up, getting the placement of the furniture just right. Then the patient sat in my chair instead of hers. And she did not come back for a second visit.

Nevertheless, by the mid 1970s I had a fellowship from the institute and a small psychotherapeutic practice. Four years later, a woman named Toby was referred to me. Neither of us knew it, but she had multiple personality disorder. Together, Toby and I discovered her internal personalities, one by one, and the abuse that caused them to be created. Working steadily for several years, we learned how to merge these alters into Toby's core personality. Eventually, she was cured and I had a new specialty. As I said, it's amazing how the unconscious mind knows just where to take you.

And then, at age 50, after a painful divorce—is there another kind?—I decided to fulfill at least part of my childhood dream. It was too late to cruise the Atlantic on a destroyer, but I could still sail my 40-footer to Bermuda. I knew that the three months I planned to take off would hurt my new career. So I decided to plan a conference for colleagues on multiple personality disorder that would take place when I got back. I hoped it would help me attract enough referrals to let me rebuild my practice.

The conference was a financial flop—it cost me and my friend and co-sponsor, Arlene Levine, $5,000 each—but a professional success. The field of multiple personality was relatively young, and therapists and patients from all over started calling me for advice and consultations. Toby and I even appeared on "60 Minutes." I wrote a book about my experiences treating patients with the disorder, *Through Divided Minds*, and more patients called. I had become an expert, at least in their eyes.

I soon developed a system for handling these multiple

personality disorder referrals. In my initial interview, I would screen the patient for post-traumatic stress disorder, the technical term for the set of conscious and unconscious behaviors by which some people deal with the effects of an especially traumatic event. I would take care to schedule the appointment for a time when it could stretch beyond the normal hour, just in case there was a spontaneous abreaction, that is, a release of the memory that had been frozen in time. Once they start, abreactions can be hard to stop.

Often hypnosis would enable me to gain access to these patients' long-buried memories. But I used other techniques as well. One of the most effective ones, I found, was to hand patients paper and crayons and ask them to draw a picture of the event. Elisabeth Kübler-Ross said that such drawings sometimes revealed more than I.Q. tests.

I became acutely sensitive to symptoms and even hints of dissociation. I learned how to question patients to uncover periods of time that were blank. One woman I saw had no memories before the age of 11. Another could not recall anything about the fifth or sixth grade, although she could remember incidents in the fourth and seventh grades. Many of these patients had some form of a sleep disturbance, such as insomnia or recurrent nightmares. Others had eating disorders, depression or anxiety. Or they resorted to alcohol, sleeping pills, marijuana or cocaine. Some suffered mood swings at unexpected times that, we later discovered, had some connection to their trauma, such as an anniversary of abusive episodes.

These patients said they had endured horrifying episodes so utterly outside the range of normal experience that they were simply intolerable to contemplate. So they banished the experiences from conscious awareness. Some would simply forget them. But others created another, separate personality to sop up the bad memory and contain it. When we are hurt, our natural response is to yell. But if for some reason we don't yell, what happens to the noise? So it is with these forgotten traumas. They lurk deep inside abuse victims, hidden pathogens that can effect their personalities and their lives.

Freud, who was the product of 19th-century scientific thinking, viewed dissociation as though it were a hydraulic system. He reasoned that energy is needed to force these traumas out of a patient's consciousness and more energy is required to keep them from seeping back into it. The result: symptoms that can include ulcers, headaches, muscle spasms, asthma, even paralysis.

These days, psychologists, invoking the more modern model of a computer, sometimes compare dissociation to a dysfunction in the storage and retrieval of information. Bad experiences are deposited in files that cannot be accessed in the normal way. But just as accidentally hitting the keyboard can cause something unintended to flash on the monitor, certain stimuli can inadvertently call up fragments of these memories. I call this flooding. It was what happened to Ned in anatomy lab. But like Ned that day, patients are exposed to only a part of the memory, not the complete experience. To discharge the trauma—and enable patients to use Freud's energy in more productive ways—I need to help them bring all of it out into their consciousness.

THIS sounds simple, but it can be an extraordinarily difficult process. Sometimes, it takes a patient years to abreact a memory, if they ever abreact it. Being abused once is bad enough. It seems unfair that to heal themselves, to recover from what someone else did to them, patients have to go through it all over again. So they resist.

Still, I had a fair amount of success coaxing abreactions from people who had been referred to me. Afterward, I would explain to them that they had just had what amounted to a psychic operation and that it would take a while to recover. Then I would send them back to their analysts for continuing treatment. The feedback I received from therapists was gratifying. Stuck cases were unstuck. Symptoms eased. Patients started getting better.

But in 20 years as a psychotherapist I hadn't encountered a patient like Rebecca. She would walk in and proceed to abreact episodes of the most outlandish abuse, usually with no prompting from me at all. Abreactions poured out of her childlike body. She would enter, nod hello, take her chair and then calmly relate—no, relive—episodes that only euphemistically could be called atrocities. She would say that pieces of these memories had come to her the night before, in dreams and flashbacks, and now she wanted to put them all together. After waiting scarcely a moment for me to nod approval—what else could I do?—she would go right into it. Rapes. Drinking blood. Eating hearts. Being used in child pornography. Being deprived of food and water for long periods. Participating in a ritual murder. Being put in a coffin with a dismembered body. To hear her tell it, there were few horrors known to man, woman or therapist she had not endured.

Abreactions came so quickly and effortlessly that it added to my already heightened suspicion about Rebecca's awful tales of abuse. I kept asking myself, are there really people in the United States who dress up in black robes, kill babies and cannibalize their hearts in some sort of pagan worship of Satan?

Indeed, Rebecca claimed that her parents' cult was connected to other groups around the country and had as members doctors, teachers, lawyers, judges and other important officials. Rebecca said she had been directed by the cult to enter a profession—she was studying criminology when she started having her disturbing flashbacks—apparently so she might eventually be helpful to the group. I suppose a criminologist might have knowledge about police procedures and therefore be able to protect the group. Rebecca said others were being trained to be nursery school teachers and day-care workers so that they could obtain children for the cult's ceremonies. Still others were encouraged to be lawyers, she said, so they could import children into the country. That was what she thought her father did. The cult also tried to encourage members to become psychiatrists who would work in mental hospitals. That way, Rebecca said, members and their children would have a safe place to go for treatment.

What frightened Rebecca—and, I might add, what also made me uncomfortable, if only when I found myself thinking that some of her outlandish recollections might be true—was the possibility that the group might discover that she was receiving psychiatric help. She was convinced members would find her. She told me she had tried to protect herself by changing her name and getting lost in New York City.

I knew all about cults such as the People's Temple, whose members committed mass suicide in Jonestown in November of 1978. I also knew that it had become a fashion among many teenagers to listen to "heavy metal" music with satanic lyrics. And I had attended conferences at which the treatment of victims of satanic cults had been discussed. Even so, it was hard for me to believe Rebecca's memories or give much credence to her fears. But I also wondered: Was I the one who was resisting? Perhaps her stories somehow reminded me of long-suppressed experiences in my own past, summoning up emotions I did not want to face and causing me to dissociate to protect myself. Or perhaps, like many people, I did not want to face the possibility that someone could have been so abused or that there are cults that hurt and kill, cults that could be so cruel to children. Even after Ned, it all just seemed farfetched.

I argued and argued and argued with myself about Rebecca. I must have re-thought her case a thousand times. I considered other psychiatric disorders. Was Rebecca malingering, deliberately feigning an illness for some other gain? Was she so internally depleted that she would pay any price, say anything, to gain my attention? That was what her previous therapist thought, and he could have been

right. Society abounds with people who bankrupt themselves to acquire status symbols that supposedly confer
peer approval. Psychological needs often overrun logic.

Was Rebecca delusional? Paranoid? The textbook defini-
tion certainly seemed to apply. She certainly had "a perva-
sive and long-standing suspiciousness and mistrust of
others." The psychiatric profession's official diagnostic
manual also refers to a "hypersensitivity" that causes someone "to constantly scan the environment for clues that
selectively validate prejudices, attitudes or biases." That
seemed to fit her as well.

But I always came back to a more likely explanation for
Rebecca's behavior: She was testing me. All psychiatric
patients test their therapists in one way or another—and
abuse victims tend to be the hardest graders. Who could
blame her for wanting to know whether I, like her previous
analyst, would turn my chair away from her?

ONE claim in particular made me most suspicious of Rebecca. She insisted that the cult had forced her to become
pregnant at least five times. She believed at least one of the
pregnancies was aborted. Her assumption was that the
others that came to term produced babies who were used in
rituals.

Rebecca retrieved memories of these pregnancies in
dribs and drabs, as was her fashion. As they surfaced, she
would go into a rage and then mourn the lost children, one
by one. She even started wearing a new piece of jewelry to
represent each of them. It was an especially difficult period
for Rebecca, who at times seemed emotionally paralyzed.
Friends stayed with her, and I visited between sessions.
Even so, she was lucky she was able to stay out of a hospital.

But she eventually gained strength, and I came to look on
the issue as an opportunity. Unlike most of her memories,
the pregnancies and childbirths presented at least some

chance for verification, and I was determined to take advantage of it. She would have been of high-school age at the time of some of the pregnancies. Surely others would know about them. Wouldn't there be hospital records of the births?

I planned my approach for weeks, then during one session very carefully began asking questions about her pregnancies. But Rebecca parried each of my forays. No one besides her family and the rest of the cult knew about them, she insisted, since she did not gain much weight and wore loose-fitting clothes. Because of her eating disorders, her weight fluctuated anyway. And she always gave birth during the summer, at her family's summer house, under the care of a physician who was a member of the group. Her one abortion came in the middle of the school year, she said, and was performed by the same physician.

Just as I was despairing of ever getting any proof, Rebecca had a yeast infection. This minor gynecological problem was another opportunity, I thought to myself. But first I had to find an acceptable physician. I had trouble tracking down doctors for other female patients who had been abused. For many, being examined by a male gynecologist was tantamount to being abused again. But just being a woman doesn't make a physician sensitive or gentle.

We finally settled on a doctor recommended by some of Rebecca's friends, and we talked about the upcoming appointment for several sessions. Our plan was that one of Rebecca's alters who had not been sexually abused would be in charge of the body during the exam. I put Rebecca in a trance, talked to the alter, who was named Darleen, and she agreed. I also talked to her internal Board of Directors, which said it would wall off the "children"—the younger and more impressionable alters—and any of the others it thought were likely to be re-traumatized by the exam. We hypnotically created a back room where all of them would wait. The Board put a watchman at the door who would make sure no one got out. And just to be safe, a female friend of Rebecca's volunteered to go along with her on the day of the appointment.

I received Rebecca's permission to talk to the doctor after the exam. She said that Rebecca had indeed been pregnant and that scar tissue made it doubtful that she could ever conceive a child again. I asked her if Rebecca's condition indicated that she had been pregnant more than once and if she had been sexually abused. The doctor said that both were possible. Then again, she quickly added, there was no way to be absolutely sure.

UNCERTAINTY is always uncomfortable, but with Rebecca I had little choice but to get used to it. If I sent her to another therapist for yet another opinion, she would assume I didn't believe her and our treatment relationship would be damaged or even destroyed. On the other hand, to fully accept what sounded so strange and could not be proven might undercut my value. After all, I was supposed to be someone grounded in reality, helping her uncover the truth. All this added to the strain of an already stressful situation.

I was also someone who was supposed to be impervious to the awful stories Rebecca and my other patients told me. I should be. I certainly have had a lot of practice. I have heard patients tell me how as girls they were raped by their fathers and warned not to tell anyone. I heard a young man describe how his father anally raped him after the boy walked into the bathroom and saw him preparing to masturbate. In one session I listened as a patient discovered that years before her father had taken her into the woods with a group of buddies who took turns molesting her.

But no matter how many of these episodes I hear, I do not get used to them. When a patient is reliving some dreadful abuse in my office, I find myself becoming sad or angry. My eyes tear. I feel rage for the perpetrator and helplessness at the injustice. And with Rebecca's case I sometimes wondered, too, what toll all this would take on me. I was working with the toxic waste of human interaction, and it seemed likely I could get infected.

The strange thing was, as I watched and listened to Rebecca while she supposedly abreacted more and more of her horrors, I was feeling less and less involved. My mind was often elsewhere. I sometimes caught myself thinking about other patients or about preparing to teach my next class. It reminded me of a summer job I had on an automobile assembly line while I was a college student. For eight hours a day I put screws in the windshields of passing cars. My body belonged to General Motors, but my mind was far from the factory.

But I was wrong. Several months after I took Rebecca on as a patient I began to have trouble with my right leg, a problem I did not associate with my strange patient until much, much later. The pain would shoot from my hip all the way to my toes and flash back again. It was difficult to find a comfortable way to sit while I worked. If I turned on that side in my sleep, the pain would wake me up.

After a full examination, my doctor sat me down and told me that as we get older we all get aches and pains. He suggested I take some aspirin and offered a prescription for sleeping pills, which, having worked for years with ex-addicts, I refused. For this, he charged my insurance company $350.

My leg still hurt, so I consulted a chiropractor. He took some X rays and told me that my spine curved in such a way that it was pressing on a nerve. He recommended a "postural realignment," which sounded like something you have done to your car after it hits a pothole. For months I went to him and he supposedly realigned my spine. His assistant taught me stretching exercises and told me to walk down the street imagining that I was a puppet held up by a string connected to the top of my head. My posture improved. My pain didn't.

Back to traditional medicine, in the person of an ortho-

pedic surgeon. After more X rays I was told that I had a
weak disk in my lower spine. I was sent to a physical
therapist, who strapped electrical contraptions onto me
that tingled unpleasantly. After a few weeks of treatments,
the pain abated, then ended altogether. But about a month
later, I awoke in the middle of the night with a piercing pain
in my right shoulder.

After another examination and still more X rays, a rheu-
matologist told me that I had osteoarthritis, which he explained was wear and tear on the joints. It was aging, he
said. There was nothing he could do.

"But the pain comes and goes," I told him. "It hits in
different spots."

"Maybe it's the weather," he replied. "Is it worse when
it's humid?"

For months I charted the weather. I never detected a
correlation.

A neurologist, my next stop, told me that I had something
called fibromyalgia syndrome, in which muscle aches are
caused by a chemical imbalance in the brain. He gave me
some medication that dried out my mouth but didn't make
the pain go away.

I was about to run out of specialists when I remembered
a physical therapist I had seen years ago for an incapacitat-
ing back spasm I suffered while waxing my boat. Arne
Nicholayeson was a 72-year-old Norwegian who was built
like a bull. He didn't believe in electronic muscle stimula-
tors. He stimulated muscles the old fashioned way—he
pummeled them.

Arne gave me a succinct diagnosis: "You're hard as a
board. You must be stressed out. What kind of work do
you do?"

For weeks he worked me over, chasing the pain from one
muscle group to another. It was like trying to fight the Viet
Cong. Hit them in one spot and they would pop up in
another. But eventually his treatment worked. I was feeling
better. The problem was, Arne wasn't. He told me that my

stress was so powerful that after he worked on my body his own would hurt.

Then, by chance, I listened to a tape from a meeting of the International Society for the Study of Multiple Personality and Dissociation. The subject: *secondary* post-traumatic stress syndrome. Some of my colleagues who were treating abused patients, it seemed, had also been suffering strange symptoms.

As I listened to the tape, I had a classic "Aha" reaction. The stories that Rebecca and Ned—but especially Rebecca—had told me were overloading my system, causing my defenses to be mobilized. Perhaps I was too sheltered. Although some part of me knew that what she and Ned described could have happened, I didn't want to believe it had happened to them. It would have made me rethink my assumptions about the world. So I denied it, and what I couldn't deny, my defenses converted to symptoms. I would talk to Arne while he manipulated my body and he got overloaded, too. Rebecca gave it to me and I gave it to Arne, who had to tread hours on a cross-country ski machine to get rid of it. God knows who got it next after Arne released it into the atmosphere.

Some other quirks I had developed made sense, too. For instance, I had the urge to discuss Rebecca's case with friends and colleagues. Obviously, I couldn't relate specific details, but I was obsessed with the subject of Satanism, which did not increase my popularity as a dinner guest. And I caught myself wondering whether some of the people I met, even old friends, belonged to secret cults.

I also had become fascinated with documentaries on World War II, the Nazis and Hitler. I was reading everything I could find on the Holocaust. In fact, I was thinking a lot about death. The death of older relatives. My own death.

I was trying, I now realize, to change my thinking. To take a harsher view of the world and human nature. Some part of me knew that I had to, in order to help Rebecca. I had to understand evil. I had to desensitize myself to brutality. I had to tolerate the emotions and feelings that these abreactions were bringing up in me. I had to stop denying them or converting them to symptoms.

To help change Rebecca, I would have to change, too.

Chapter 7

EDUCATION
IN EVIL

MY musical tastes range across a wide spectrum, but not wide enough for what the MTV crowd calls heavy metal. Still, I was aware that these ear-shattering arrangements sometimes featured lyrics with satanic themes. At Kean College, where I teach, the administration was sufficiently concerned about its influence to ban this music from the campus radio station. And the tabloids and the television news programs often had accounts of heavy-metal fans who caused all sorts of trouble, desecrating cemeteries, churches and synagogues with occult symbols and, sometimes, holding sacrificial rites with neighborhood pets. The experts usually regarded them as dabblers who picked up a little satanic theory and used it to express their rebellion. It seemed likely that drugs, at least as much as beliefs, fueled their behavior.

But from time to time I also read about more troubled souls who killed themselves or others, insisting they were acting at Satan's behest. In 1989, 15 bodies were found at a ranch 20 miles west of Matamoros, across the border from Brownsville, Texas. Nearly all were ritually killed and mutilated. (One had his spinal column removed and used for a necklace.) The Mexican police also found a squat iron kettle containing dried blood and charred animal and human remains. They pieced together a tale of a devil-worshiping cult of drug smugglers who believed human sacrifice would guarantee protection for their marijuana business.

A few months after Matamoros, the authorities discovered several bodies at a farmhouse near Toledo, Ohio, who were said to be sacrificial victims of another satanic cult.

Such cases seem to crop up every so often, but I had never thought much about them. Now, after listening to Ned and then Rebecca, I saw them in a more frightening light. It still seemed possible—probable?—that my patients were exaggerating. But, of course, I couldn't be sure it didn't happen as they only hazily remembered. After all, it apparently *had* happened in Mexico and in Ohio and who knows where else.

A FEW days after Rebecca's abreaction, I was sitting in front of the computer terminal in the Kean College library, thinking what a shame it was that the marvelous black box hadn't been around when I was in graduate school. I would have been spared long hours spent thumbing through worn card catalogues and Readers' Guides. Now, it was simply a matter of accessing databases in psychology, anthropology, sociology, history and medicine. I typed in some search words—devil, devil worship, ritual abuse, Satanism and satanic cults—and in a few minutes I had 20 dot-matrix pages summarizing some 50 articles.

The first on my list was "An Empirical Study of Wiccan Religion in Postindustrial Society." A wiccan is a modern "white" witch, I learned, the kind who worship benign, pre-Christian goddesses. ("Black" witches are the ones who worship Satan.) The article was based on responses to a questionnaire mailed to the editors of 76 pagan journals and the leaders of 260 pagan churches in North America. That seemed like a lot of pagan journals and churches. Apparently, there was a world here that I did not know existed.

I scanned some of the other summaries: "Sacrifice and the Experience of Power," "Sacrifices Involving Large Livestock in the North Thailand Highlands" and "Nihilistic Adolescents, Heavy Metal Rock Music and Paranormal Beliefs." "Nouveau Witches" noted that white witchcraft thrived during economic recessions. An article from a journal from India described the songs of the Kondh, which once accompanied rites of human sacrifice the group long ago gave up. I learned that in 1982 there was a colloquium in Paris on "The Uses of the Occult, Magic and Witchcraft in American Culture." Why in Paris? I wondered.

My excitement with this trove of research faded as I realized there was much more on Satanism in the sociological and anthropological literature than in the medical and psychological journals—and even more, of course, in the popular press. I had hoped to find reports from colleagues who had treated patients who said that they, like Ned and Rebecca, had been subjected to ritual abuse. I was looking for cases I could study, cases that would tell me how to proceed. There were none.

Before I left the library, I sought out a copy of the New York City Yellow Pages near the telephone bank. One of the wonderful things about New York is that it has at least one of everything. I checked under "Occult" and found a promising entry: Samuel Weiser Inc., a bookstore at 132 East 24th Street, not far from my apartment.

It turned out to be a pleasant old shop on the south side of a tree-lined street, with bookshelves divided into sections on astrology, kabala, tarot cards, the I Ching, crystal-ball gazing, numerology and so on. It all somehow reminded me of the 1960s, when I spent several years in Big Sur, California, of girls in long, billowing skirts and visits to the Phoenix bookstore, in the basement of the Nepenthe restaurant that was in a converted house Howard Hughes built for Rita Hayworth on a cliff overlooking the Pacific.

My California daydream was interrupted when I came to the section on Satanism. Nestled on the shelves was a seven-volume study by a historian at the University of California, Jeffrey Burton Russell. It looked to be the definitive work on the subject. I spent $300 for about 20 books, including Russell's prodigious effort. I would start, as I so often do, with the past.

IT didn't take much reading to arrive at the conclusion that rituals similar to those we now associate with Satanism have been reported by every society for which we have records. There is also an increasing amount of archeological evidence that earlier cultures engaged in such practices as ritual sacrifice, which has probably been going on since our ancestors stopped munching fruits and berries and began competing with other predators for protein-rich flesh.

For primitive man, the African savannah was an unpredictable and terrifying environment. These hunters and gatherers faced a life of feast or famine, sickness or health, all at the discretion of forces beyond their control. Appease the gods and they might survive, or at least save themselves from a clobbering. And the most powerful form of appeasement was the gift of what they held most dear: life itself.

Early man did not view death as we have come to regard it. Death was natural, not so much an end as a pause before a new beginning. They learned this from nature. They watched the sun die in the evening and be reborn in the morning. They watched plants die, turn to mulch and sustain new growth. "Out of the rocks of fallen wood and leaves, fresh sprouts arise, from which the lesson appears to have been that from death springs life, and out of death new birth," wrote the scholar Joseph Campbell. "And the grim conclusion drawn was that the way to increase life is to increase death. Accordingly, the entire equatorial belt of this globe has been characterized by a frenzy of sacrifice—vegetable, animal and human sacrifice."

To increase life, increase death. Primitive man surely knew this. Population control was essential to hunters and gatherers, who could feed only so many. Was natural death enough? What happened to the old and infirm, who could no longer support themselves? What happened in the case of multiple births, which threw off the already marginal demographics of the tribe? There were no foundling homes for unwanted or unhealthy Stone-Age children. Certainly some must have been abandoned. Nor does it seem unreasonable that some were also killed—sacrificed—to sustain the life of the group. And once sacrifice is accepted in one context, it can be used by others for darker purposes.

In the same vein, the many admonitions against human sacrifice and the drinking of blood in the Bible seem an indication of the existence, if not the prevalence, of these practices in the Mesopotamian culture from which our society emerged. The Bible also describes the barbaric rites of the idolatrous pagans who lived in Canaan and sacrificed children to Baal, their fertility god. And the prophet Jeremiah spoke of a shrine at Topheth, in the valley of Ben-Hinnom, at which children were burned.

The Hebrews of the Old Testament tried to transform this primitive practice. Some scholars believe that Deuteronomy, the book of law, was partially motivated by the desire to replace human sacrifice with animal sacrifice. Moral considerations aside, animal sacrifice was more useful economically, since the slaughter by the affluent of their cattle in a religious ceremony ensured that the poor would be able to eat.

But were the Hebrews really so much different from their neighbors? Some scholars wonder. Consider the story in which God directs Abraham to sacrifice his son, Isaac. Abraham takes Isaac to the mountain, places him on the altar and is about to begin when an angel intervenes, saying that since Abraham has unquestionably obeyed, Isaac is to be spared. But was it the angel or perhaps a later biblical editor who stayed Abraham's hand?

And hundreds of years later didn't Moses, the lawgiver, try to sacrifice his son on his way to Egypt, to ensure the success of his mission? His wife, Zipporah, intervened, cutting off the child's foreskin as a substitute for the boy's life.

In the rituals Ned and Rebecca reported, there was copious use of blood—they were forced to drink it and it was poured over them and other victims. The subject made me feel ill, even though I like sushi and steak tartare. But I learned in my reading that the ceremonial use of blood also has historical antecedents. The Hebrews viewed blood as sacred. Some believe that they, like the members of Mesopotamian cultures, used blood in their rituals, bathing in it, dashing it at the base of their altars and sprinkling it in their sanctuaries.

Today, archeological finds are correlating with many of the references to sacrifices in the Bible, as well as other "myths." On the north coast of Africa, opposite Sicily, altars have been found with human remains that are similar to ones described in the Bible. At the Palace of Knossos, on the Mediterranean island of Crete, archaeologists have found more altars and burial urns—evidence that human sacrifice was practiced by the highly advanced Minoan civilization that flourished from 3000 B.C. to 1100 B.C. So in other cultures—highly regarded cultures—sacrifice was widespread.

*   *   *

As they assembled their empire, the Romans incorporated all the gods they encountered, such as Osiris, the Egyptian god of fertility, and Dionysus, the Greek god of wine, who inspired celebrations in which adherents would run down the streets, tearing animals and people limb from limb. And as Christianity in turn supplanted the Roman religions, the Christians confronted the problem of what to do with the pagan gods the Romans had absorbed. These gods were relics of old religions that were familiar and organic, following nature and glorifying sexuality. But the Christians were moving in the opposite direction, toward the denial of the flesh. They resolved the dilemma the same way the Romans did, by adopting another entity, the devil. Christianity's phenomenal success can partly be attributed to its ability to adapt themes and practices from these older sects. "The early church was an organism that fed upon the whole pagan world, selecting and incorporating a wide variety of ideas and practices," wrote the historian Edward McNall Burns. "The appeal of Christianity was therefore more nearly universal than that of any other of the ancient religions."

Among the ideas Christianity incorporated from the pagans were that death begets life and that sacrifice will be rewarded. Both ideas were transmitted through the central belief, the Christ story. The Eucharist, celebrated at the Catholic Mass in which the wafer and wine are symbolically transformed into the body and blood of Christ, is a representation of these themes.

But if the more brutal customs were filtered out as the pagans were absorbed by Christianity, it seems reasonable to assume that some of these practices continued among various groups of heretics and outsiders. Did some drink blood and eat flesh? Was it a coincidence that the Mithraists, one of the popular religions of the late Roman empire that survived the Christian transformation, celebrated their holy day by killing a bull, drinking his blood and eating his flesh, as a symbol of resurrection? Was it coincidence that their holy day, December 25, was the date assigned for the birth of Christ?

Eventually the Christians, in order to spare their loving, forgiving God from being blamed for the evil that happens in the world, split Him in two, following the Persian dualistic strain of which Zoroastrianism is the best known example. Now they could explain evil; the physical world was under control of the evil deity, Satan. But in so doing, the Christians gave form and power to the modern idea of Satan and created an alternative to turn to in times of stress or frustration.

As Christianity grew, it was beset by schisms that would lead centuries later to its fracture and the emergence of Protestantism. In an attempt to combat the disunity, Christian leaders preached asceticism and blamed the devil for tempting people into evil practices. They made their religion more and more restrictive and austere. And as they did so, more and more people rebelled. I am not an expert in this area, even though I have taught Western Civilization for years, but it seems logical to me that satanic practices—worshiping the Antichrist rather than Christ—were used in this rebellion.

In the 13th century the church persecuted people it considered to be witches, accusing them of devil worship. In the 14th century, members of the Knights Templar, a fraternal organization of Crusaders, were accused of practicing Satanism and imprisoned. But the church's strictness brought more opposition. Among the splinter groups were the Luciferians, a sect that worshiped Lucifer as the bringer of light. Soon, Christian rebels and members of various neopagan groups were holding what came to be known as Black Masses, which were blasphemous, orgiastic parodies of the Catholic Mass. Satan, not God, was the object of worship, and the chalice would contain blood or even excrement rather than wine.

In the 15th century there were several prominent cases of individuals who practiced varieties of what might be called Satanism. The best known was that of Gilles de Rais, a.k.a. Bluebeard, who was burned at the stake after a chapel, complete with inverted cross, black candles and altar, was found at his home. There was a statue of a hideous demon, presumably Satan. One room contained copper vessels filled with the blood of his sacrificial victims, bearing neat labels with the dates of their execution. He confessed to eight slayings in all. It reminded me too much of the stories I heard from Ned and Rebecca.

During the scientific revolution of the 18th century, Satan underwent a metamorphosis from godhead to carnival freak and plaything of aristocratic rakes searching for a neo-religious creed to justify sexual perversion. Members of the infamous Hellfire Clubs, which appeared in 1730 in Ireland and later in England, would dress as devils and hold satanic rituals, with processions of white-and-red-robed monks carrying torches, black candles and inverted crucifixes. They would use a naked woman as their altar and drink sacrificial wine from her navel.

Devil worship was given another boost into public awareness when Aleister Crowley, an English author, poet and adventurer, invented and preached a complex unholy alliance that synthesized Satanism, Eastern mysticism, Tantric yoga and Jewish Kabalism, using these religions as an excuse for hedonism. He formed an organization called the Hermetic Order of the Golden Dawn whose members—including William Butler Yeats and Bram Stoker—performed orgiastic rituals in clubs that flourished until the 1920s. Crowley was supposedly trying to attain the godhead through excess, especially sexual excess. He also ingested every hallucinogen then known. He died in 1947, impoverished and addicted.

In the cultural and political turbulence of the 1960s many members of a generation alienated by technology and Vietnam turned to drugs, Eastern philosophy and the occult. A new satanic revival blossomed, spurred along by Anton LaVey, founder of the First Church of Satan in San Francisco and author of The Satanic Bible, which sold more than 500,000 copies. Very much in the Crowley tradition, LaVey believed that Satan "represents indulgence, instead of abstinence" and "vengeance, instead of turning the other cheek."

His "bible" is partly a criticism of conventional religion and modern morality, both of which he regards as hypocritical. It is also a how-to guide to satanic ritual, including instructions on what to wear (black hooded robes for men, sexier outfits for women), what symbolic objects to have on hand (bells to open and close the ceremony and gongs to call the forces of darkness) and the proper altar (preferably a naked woman, because Satanism is a religion of the flesh).

He is careful to say that no one is physically or sexually abused. He is also careful to say that even though some people think the sacrifice of a living being increases the power of the ceremony, it is not necessary and he does not condone it. Satanism, he asserts, has been given a bad name through its association with the Black Mass, although he does provide a description of that ceremony:

"A defrocked priest stands before an altar consisting of a nude woman, her legs spread-eagled and vagina thrust open, each of her outstretched fists grasping a black candle made from the fat of unbaptized babies, and a chalice containing the urine of a prostitute (or blood) reposing on her belly. An inverted cross hangs above the altar, and triangular hosts of ergot-laden bread of black-stained turnip are methodically blessed as the priest dutifully slips them in and out of the altar-lady's labia. Then, we are told, an invocation to Satan and various demons is followed by an array of prayers and psalms chanted backwards or interspersed with obscenities . . . all performed within the confines of a 'protective' pentagram drawn on the floor. If the devil appears, he is invariably in the form of a rather eager man wearing the head of a black goat upon his shoulders. Then follows a potpourri of flagellation, prayer-book burning, cunnilingus, fellatio, and general hindquarters kissing—all done to a background of ribald recitations from the Holy Bible and audible expectorations on the cross! If a baby can be slaughtered during the ritual, so much the better; for as everyone knows, this is the favorite sport of the Satanist!"

Some Satanists also engage in debaptisms, which supposedly undo Christian baptisms, and attend catechism classes in which adherents are taught satanic symbols that either ridicule the corresponding Christian ones or have roots in ancient cultures supposedly stamped out by the Christians. Some Satanists believe in an elaborate system of numerology built around the number six. (The Book of Revelation, 13:18, says: "Let him that hath understanding count the number of the beast; for it is the number of man; and his number is six hundred three score and six." Any multiple of six can be important.) Certain dates can also have special significance, including those of ancient pagan festivals and rituals—for example, October 31, or Halloween, which was a Druid festival—or dates celebrating plantings and harvests or seasonal changes, such as the solstices and equinoxes.

Satanists are known to chant and dance in a circle. In occult lore, sorcerers protected themselves from evil spirits by retreating inside a magic circle. Some Satanists wear animal masks, a practice traced to the pagans, who worshiped the animals they killed to live.

Modern Satanism, by most accounts, is diverse and disorganized, embraced by a wide range of practitioners whose number is anyone's guess. At the very least, Satanism would seem to be an effective way to rebel against established values, which probably explains most of the teenage dabblers who take drugs and scream "Hail Satan" at heavy-metal concerts. In my generation, it was a fad to see how many people you could stuff in a phone booth. In my Greenwich Village neighborhood now, it is in vogue to dress like the Wicked Witch of the West.

Pleasure is also a reward. Satanism provides followers with a chance to engage in hedonistic excesses that the rest of us view as immoral, if not illegal.

Undoubtedly some dabblers graduate from mere mischief to, say, desecrating a church or cemetery. Or they join similarly minded individuals to conduct rituals that often seem designed to put practitioners into an altered, even hypnotic, state, in which sensual experiences are enhanced and moral and psychological constraints diminished. Could that account for the stories I heard from Ned and Rebecca about rape, torture, human sacrifice and cannibalism?

IT was getting dark as I walked crosstown to the Magickal Childe, another occult bookstore I learned about in one of the books I bought in Weiser's. It was narrow and dimly lit. I squeezed through its crowded aisles, passing people browsing through books on all sort of occult subjects. In the back, a woman dressed in Merlin-like robes sat at a bridge table and offered to read tarot cards.

I was considering a consultation when a nearby display caught my eye. It contained apothecary jars filled with various roots, herbs and berries. I recognized some of them from my years in pharmacy school and from when as a teenager I worked in my uncle's drugstore and sold some of the same substances to people who used them in potions or hung them around their necks to ward off the fever. Next to the display was another glass case. I walked over and stared. There, against black felt, were daggers, swords, silver chalices and robes. There were knives made of silver and gold, or good imitations of them. Some had jeweled handles. Some had curved blades. They looked menacing.

I stood in front of the daggers and knives for a while,

thinking about Ned and Rebecca. I was still hesitant to accept it. Could there possibly be such evil?

My doubts put me in good company. Freud had the same problem. He could not accept that so many of his patients had been sexually abused, preferring to believe that as children they wished to have sex with their fathers or mothers. This may be true in many cases, but we now have estimates that as many as one in four females and one in five males have been sexually abused as children. For generations we have blamed the victims, perhaps because we could not face the evil tendencies in ourselves. Was that what I was doing by questioning Rebecca now?

I may never know the truth about Rebecca, I thought to myself. But for the moment, at least, it didn't matter. Rebecca was suffering, and she was my patient.

Chapter 8

HELEN

IT was hard to believe that such an intelligent person, with degrees from Smith and Stanford, could be so difficult. That Helen was a psychotherapist made it all the more frustrating. She was a large-framed woman in her early 30s, with dark brown hair and olive skin. Helen always wore man-tailored business suits, usually dark, but with sneakers. Her business shoes, unsuitable for the streets of New York or the subway stairs, were in her shoulder bag.

Helen had sought me out eight years earlier to treat one of her friends. Then she watched me work with this patient for five years before she herself started therapy with me. But once we began, her every action seemed calculated to avoid making progress, if not alienate me. She was the exact opposite of Rebecca, who would begin to have an abreaction almost as soon as she arrived in my office, with scarcely any prompting. Something made Helen want to sabotage my every effort to help her.

Helen had several creative ways to forestall the work of therapy, including picking fights with me or always having a crisis handy that demanded our immediate attention. But her standby was chronic lateness, when she didn't cancel our appointments altogether.

I admit I made some errors with Helen. My major mistake was to assume that she would be psychologically astute, since she was a therapist, too. I remember one day in particular. She burst through my door with only five minutes left in her hour. I thought by simply pointing out her lateness might be therapeutic resistance that she, as an analyst, might be willing to examine her behavior.

She wasn't. In fact, she went into a tirade. Didn't she seek me out? she almost yelled at me. Didn't she keep coming, even though I kept making incorrect interpretations? Would a patient who was resisting treatment do all that?

Backpedaling to save the session, I apologized for even mentioning the word resistance, which prompted another argument over what the term really meant. Helen insisted that I was the one who was resisting, by focusing on her lateness. What was the problem? she wanted to know. All she had done was talk too long on the telephone to a friend, causing her to be a little late. "I just couldn't hang up on her," she declared. "I was waiting for her call all week."

I felt defeated, angry and frustrated. "Cut it out already," I wanted to say to her. "Don't you know we're on the same side?" Fortunately, I didn't say anything. I simply settled back in my chair and waited for her abbreviated session to end.

From then on I avoided confronting Helen over her lateness, or any of the other manifestations of her resistance. Instead of using our time together to get at more substantial problems, our sessions were filled with relatively routine complaints about, in approximate order of frequency: her boyfriend, me, her mother, her sister, her boss, and construction workers who made rude comments when she walked by them on the street. It really didn't matter which item she was complaining about. The message was always the same. Someone had done her wrong. And during those rare times when most of her relationships were going well, and no one was hassling her on the street, she would complain about the weather. She did not feel well in hot weather. Or cold weather. The weather could ruin her entire day.

About half of our sessions were devoted to problems with her boyfriends. They changed with some regularity, but that did not help. They all seemed the same—the bastard of a thousand faces. These selfish, childish men would make impossible demands. They would force her to have sex. They would lie about other women or about being married. They fought with her, sometimes physically. They took advantage of what she thought was her generous nature. When I would suggest that she negotiate for her rights and set limits, she would listen attentively, then insist that she just couldn't do it. She never really wanted to examine why she allowed herself to stay in what she knew were destructive liaisons. She just wanted to complain.

It was even worse when Helen did not have a boyfriend. A breakup would always lead to a deep depression. Sometimes she would talk about suicide, and in a few instances I had to send her to a psychiatrist for antidepressant medication. But it would take about six weeks for the medication to begin to work, and by then Helen would usually have found a new boyfriend. And then, of course, complaints would begin all over again.

I would have dismissed Helen simply as being spoiled if she hadn't stated upon entering treatment that she suspected she had been sexually abused as a child. She hazily recalled one episode during her teenage years when she believed her father came into her bed. Then her memory went blank, she said.

Talking with Helen during my initial interview, I realized that she could not remember large chunks of her childhood. And there was another, classic clue that made me suspicious: she told me that she sometimes found different brands of cigarettes in her purse.

Yet she would never let me investigate these symptoms or discuss her suspicions about her father. When I tried to push her, she would tell me how confused she was. And then she would begin complaining about other things.

After a few months, Helen's refusal to confront what I believed were probably childhood traumas grew increasingly frustrating for me. But I didn't know how to help her face them. Arnold, my supervisor in analytic school, used to say that much of therapy was simply waiting for a break. "Just keep the process going," was his mantra. "Sooner or later, something will happen."

Just when I was beginning to despair that Helen would wear me out before the process wore her down, the break finally came. Helen had arrived at my office in a particularly nasty mood. She noticed that I had purchased a new couch and went into a rage, accusing me of trying to drive her out of therapy. Didn't I know that she liked the old couch? Didn't I know that she needed to have everything remain the same? This was the only safe place she had in the world, she hissed, and now I had destroyed it. She accused me of not liking her. She accused me of having a "massive negative transference." (One of the problems taking on analysts as patients is that they can turn the jargon against you.)

It was the same old resistance; external events were once again the source of her difficulty. If only the world would change, then she would get better. I found myself getting angrier and angrier. It reminded me of the times in my life when I had tried to please my mother and failed. There just wasn't anything I could do to please Helen.

While she was berating me about the couch, I started to fantasize about constructing a glass wall between us that would protect me from her venom. Drifting off into my own inner world, I remembered an incident in my childhood when I fell down a hill in Verona Lake, New Jersey, and cut my head. I was rushed to the hospital for stitches. I don't think I have ever been happier than I was when I finally returned home. As I thought about this, a phrase popped into my mind: Underneath anger is pain.

I caught Helen's gaze squarely.

"You must be in terrible pain to be so angry with me over the couch," I said.

Her tirade stopped. Her expression softened, and she lowered her head and began to cry. After a few moments, she composed herself and told me a story. She had gone to her health club the previous night, put her clothes in a locker and went through her usual exercise routine. When she went back to her locker, it was empty and the lock was gone. She searched down the row of lockers and found the lock on another locker a few feet away. Her clothes were inside.

I thought about those different brands of cigarettes she found in her purse. My suspicions of multiplicity were heightened. I hoped that Helen was worried enough about the episode in the health club to let me investigate it. As Freud said, only two things motivate people, love and pain. We now had the pain.

I suggested to Helen that she might have had a dissociative experience and that if she allowed me to hypnotize her we might be able to unravel it. For the first time since she entered therapy, she agreed to let me put her into a trance.

As soon as she was under, I asked Helen if there were other people inside her. Yes, she told me right away, there were three such people: Helena was about Helen's age; Meg and Alice were six and nine, respectively.

I asked to speak to Helena and she came right out. After a few moments of small talk, I brought up the curious health-club incident. Helena admitted that she had moved the clothes. She did it, she said, to make a point to Helen.

"I was getting fed up with her," Helena said. "All she does is complain. I try and talk to her, but she won't listen to me. She tries to drown me out or claims not to hear me. I had to do something extreme to get her attention, to get her to deal with things. She's not getting better. You haven't had much success, so I tried."

I sat there, smiling to myself. After months of frustration, this was too good to be true.

I asked Helena whether there were any others inside besides the two young girls. She said there was another group of personalities, but that I didn't want to meet them yet. I decided to let this go for now, since the session was almost over. I brought Helen back and took her out of the trance.

"Then that explains it," she said after I told her what had just gone on. She was shaken, yet relieved.

"I never wanted to accept it. But I knew. On some level, I knew. It explains a lot of things. Especially the voices in my head that I couldn't tell you about. And dreams that I have been having."

I sat quietly through all this, occasionally nodding. Usually, the accessing of internal alters and the making of a diagnosis calms a patient and at the same time points up the seriousness of the situation. Usually, it also leads to the uncovering of the abusive situations that had caused the multiplicity. I was confident Helen and I had at last reached a turning point.

BUT we hadn't. When Helen came for her next appointment, she told me she had a fight with her boss and had lost her job. For weeks she was consumed with the job hunt, with writing résumés and going to interviews. She also worried incessantly about money, not that I blamed her. New York is expensive, especially for an unemployed person in therapy. But these concerns filled up all of our moments together, making it impossible to progress any further in examining her multiplicity.

And when she was again working as a therapist, this time in a city agency, the old resistance returned in full force.

Her chronic lateness resumed and she would cancel sessions, giving only the flimsiest of excuses.

As in the past, if I so much as mentioned this resistance I was accused of not understanding her. She would not let me hypnotize her. And she now denied Helena even existed.

I kept chipping away at the resistance, waiting for another break. At times it was almost unbearably frustrating listening to her complaints. I knew they served to take the focus of therapy away from the abuse I believed lurked in her past. But every so often there would be a short period in which she would allow a few childhood memories to surface. Once she recalled going to a cemetery after a relative's funeral and being left there. Another time, her father went into a rage and killed her pet terrier. She also told me about some of her dreams. A few contained images of candles and robes.

There were other intriguing indications that I was on the right path. At one session, I asked her to quickly jot down the 10 things that most frightened her. Helen's list included blood, black, red, candles, knives, coffins and ghosts. And by keeping careful treatment notes, I realized that Helen often mentioned that she became anxious at dates other patients told me coincided with the ancient pagan festivals and ceremonies, such as Halloween and the winter and summer solstices.

From all this, I was beginning to suspect that Helen was not only an abused patient but also might be a victim of ritual abuse—the same sort of abuse Rebecca claimed to have endured. But each new tidbit of information was followed by a new period of resistance. The pattern was rigid. Helen would arrive late, stretch her long frame out on the couch and complain about some mundane problem. Somehow or other we would resolve it. After a few weeks her life would become quiet and she would begin to open up about some abusive episode in her childhood. But as we would start to explore it, another everyday difficulty would arise and fill our next few sessions. Complaint, resolution, start of a memory, complaint again. That was the cycle. My problem: How could we break it?

I thought about a workshop I attended given by Drs. Roberta Sachs and Corydon Hammond at a previous meeting of the International Society for the Study of Multiple Personality and Dissociation. The subject was hypnotic techniques for patients with multiple personality disorder, and one of their ideas was to have the patient create an internal "safe room" within which she could let herself deal with threatening issues. They suggested putting the patient in a trance, then having her walk down an imaginary flight of stairs to the basement, then down a hall to a door that was locked. Only the patient had the key. She could go into the room and lock the door behind her. No one could bother her there.

Hypnotic subjects take things very literally. Believing that they were safe in such a room, they could talk about episodes they would not ordinarily discuss. I liked Sachs and Hammond's induction, too, especially the way in which they led the patient "down the stairs" and "down the hall." The imagery made it seem like they were somehow submerging into the subconscious recesses of their patient's mind, where the memories reside.

I told Helen about the pattern I had noticed in our sessions—that whenever we got close to a memory, or she started to talk about her childhood, a crisis would conveniently occur in her life that would need attention. Then I made a suggestion. We should schedule an extra session and use it only to explore her past. I was surprised how little coaxing it took to win her agreement.

On the appointed day, Helen showed up late. I wasn't surprised. Rather than risk a fight, I simply told her I was glad she was here. I had already decided that I would use a hypnotic induction that was geared toward reminding her of when she was perhaps five or six. I hoped it would help bring us back to Helen's missing years.

"Let your eyes focus on something in front of you," I told her. "Stare at it while you listen to me talk.

"When you were young and learning to read, you probably had a lot of difficulty with your letters. Most of us did. It was hard for you to tell the difference between a "b" and a "d," a "p" and a "q," an "m" and an "n." At some point you formed a mental picture of each letter. Your mind knew what each letter looked like and that allowed you to tell the difference and re-create it whenever you wanted to. By now you have formed a mental picture of whatever you have been staring at, and you can re-create that in your mind's eye.

"Close your eyes," I went on. "Now, in your mind's eye you can see the object that you were looking at. If you hear sounds outside, you can listen to them or let them pass through your mind. You may even choose not to hear them. You will hear my voice. My voice will go with you wherever you go. You will always stay in contact with my voice."

I could see her expression soften.

"See yourself walking down a beautiful staircase, Helen. It has a solid bannister to hold onto. That's right, a step at a time, you go down, down to the bottom. There is a long hallway. You walk down the hallway. At the end is a door with a big lock. Only you have the key. Now take the key out. Open the door and go inside. Lock the door. See yourself very safe, very protected. No one can bother you in this room. You can talk to me and hear my voice."

I waited a moment.

"Helen, are you in your room?"

"Yes," she said faintly.

"Do you feel safe?"

"No."

"No?"

"No." Her voice was firm. "This room is not safe. They can still get me."

Fighting my surprise and discouragement, I tried to join her resistance.

"Okay, Helen, maybe we can make some changes to make the room safe. I'll make some suggestions. Do them if you feel that they are right, and do anything else you want, too."

She didn't seem very enthusiastic.

"Let's back the door up with steel," I suggested. "That will make it very strong, so no one can break it down."

I paused a moment.

"Now let's take out any windows and put in closed-circuit television cameras, so you can see what's outside. Let's put two big guard dogs at the entrance. They'll keep everyone else out. Have you done all that?"

"Yes."

"How do you feel now?"

"I still don't feel safe. They can still get me. They can kill the dogs and use a blowtorch to burn through the door. There is no place that is safe."

I can't say I was really surprised. I have read books in which famous therapists reveal how they cure patients. I try the same things in my office. Sometimes they work, and sometimes they don't.

Helen was still in a trance. I decided to try a technique that I had already tested.

"I know that you were probably told that something bad would happen to you if you told anyone what happened to you when you were a child. If that is true, I don't think that you should tell anyone now. After all, your safety is the most important thing. But maybe you could write me a story about it. Or perhaps someone inside you could write about what happened."

I gave her a yellow pad and a blue felt-tip pen and waited.

She picked the pen up and started to write furiously. It

took me a few seconds to realize that Helen was using her left hand even though she was right-handed. I looked over her shoulder at the pad. Helen had written: "She needs safety. Do not be discouraged. The Evil One does not want us to tell."

"Who is the Evil One?" I asked.

"He is from the other group," she wrote. "We do not talk to him. We avoid him. We are not supposed to tell."

"What are you not supposed to tell?"

"Need Protection," the left hand wrote back.

"How can we protect her?"

"Keep the Evil One away."

"Who is the Evil One?"

"Very evil," the hand wrote.

"What does the Evil One do?"

"Evil."

"What kind of evil?"

"Can't tell you."

I thought of the most evil thing any of my ritually abused patients had told me about.

"Does the Evil One do bad things to children?"

Helen's body jolted upright and her brown hair swung back. I had hit a nerve. But as I was congratulating myself, Helen suddenly jumped out of the chair and lunged at me, using the pen as a dagger.

My right arm went up, blocking hers. She dropped the pen and, with both of her hands, went for my throat. Her face flushed red, but she was utterly silent. I grabbed her by the wrists and twisted hard, forcing her to the floor. She continued to struggle so, a proper analytic intervention not coming to my mind, I sat on her. After a few moments she became calm, and her eyes took on a vacant stare.

I looked down at her, afraid she would resume struggling. I didn't know what to do. This had never happened before. My heart was racing. I never touch patients, much less wrestle with them. I couldn't think of what to do. I knew I couldn't keep sitting on her.

She had been hypnotized when she came at me. Perhaps I could push her further back into the trance.

"Deeper and deeper," I said as calmly as I could. "Deeper and deeper, Helen. Deeper and deeper."

I saw her start to relax. I kept repeating the phrase. Eventually, she became limp and her head drooped. I cautiously got off her and backed away. The forces of health were stronger than those on the other side, I thought to myself. Or maybe I had just gotten lucky.

I assumed that another internal personality attacked me. I addressed all of her personalities at once, or at least tried to. "Bring Helen back now," I demanded.

I waited for what seemed like a very long time. Then I noticed her face relax even more. Tentatively, I asked: "Helen, is that you?"

"Yes."

Thank God, I thought to myself. "Now, please stand up and go back to the chair."

She crossed the room, smoothing her skirt and jacket in a fragile gesture before she lowered herself into the bent-wood chair.

I picked up the pen and the yellow pad and told her to take a few minutes in the trance to calm down. Then I brought her out of it.

"How do you feel?"

"Strange." she said. "I feel relaxed, but tired. Exhausted. My body aches. I want to go home."

"Do you remember what happened?"

"Some. It's very foggy. I remember about the room. I remember that it was hard to feel safe. But that's all. What else was there?"

I decided to buy time with a half truth.

"We did some investigation into your past, Helen, but obviously you're not ready to remember it just yet. I think it's best you go home and rest. We'll talk more about it next time."

Helen agreed, and on slightly shaky legs she left my

office. I noticed I was trembling. I knew I had triggered something, but I didn't know what.

I should have paid more attention to the resistance and not tried to push through it, I thought. Hadn't I learned from Ned? This time, I had been lucky.

Chapter 9

"DANCE FOR THE MEN"

I was careful not to show any skepticism about the stories Rebecca told me, no matter how gruesome or improbable they seemed. And she seemed to be responding to treatment like a garden after a wet spring.

When Rebecca first entered therapy with me, her friends all came from the incest-support group. Now, she was starting to reach out to old friends and make new ones, getting to know people who were not abuse victims. She was working one night a week in a shelter for homeless people and donating time to several other social causes. She was even dating.

The character of our sessions changed, too. Rebecca was spending less time reliving satanic episodes and more time discussing her internal world. I was meeting all sorts of new alters. Some of them told me they had been neglected for years. There were several lesbian alters, for example, who were upset whenever Rebecca had a relationship with a male. But there were also heterosexual alters who liked her to have an active social life, except when she had an affair with a female.

In fact, Rebecca's increasingly crowded internal world was sometimes bristling with conflict, and when there was conflict very little therapeutic work would get done, since our time would be spent resolving the disputes. Religious alters wanted to go to temple, which made the internal atheists uncomfortable. There also were arguments over what to wear, where to go on vacation, what to watch on television.

I realized I had to help Rebecca set up a system of mediation if we were ever going to integrate all the aspects of her personality. The solution I hit upon was a parliament. Under hypnosis, I helped Rebecca create an internal meeting hall large enough to accommodate all of her alters. We called it the General Assembly. There was a long table at one end for the Board of Directors. At its head sat the Chairman, whom I still had not met.

Time was allotted once a week for a general meeting, at which any alter with a problem was free to voice it. Solutions would be proposed and the entire group would vote. It seemed to work most of the time. When there was a dispute over how her apartment would be redecorated, for instance, the decision was that areas would be allocated to each group of alters, who in term would assign sections to subgroups. It made for what Rebecca described as a kind of Victorian hodgepodge, but at least it was a peaceful hodgepodge.

Occasionally, though, there were problems that the parliament could not resolve. Some were caused by an alter named Mary, who insisted on working in a topless bar near Ned's favorite neighborhood, Times Square, making life miserable for some of the other alters who had been abused. They became terrified when men would try to paw Mary or stuff a bill in her G-string. (Even I felt a little bit concerned. Some of these places could be dangerous.) But when they asked Mary to stop dancing, she angrily refused. She needed the money, she said. And anyway, she enjoyed dancing, and maybe even being pawed. It was the only chance she had to be out in the real world, Mary said. And the power and control she felt over the men in the audience was a thrill.

"Do you believe it?" Mary told me when I talked to her about it. "They come in after working all week and spend all that money. And they get nothing out of it."

"How does it work?" I asked.

"It's simple. I dance, and they watch." She had a smug look. "I make money just by doing what I like to do. Sometimes I notice who's trying to make eye contact with me. I have a knack for picking the right one. I look him right in the eye and then I dance just for him. He offers me more money and in my softest voice I thank him and gently touch his fingers as I take it. If I've picked the right one, he's gone. He'll keep tipping me. When he's played out, I'll move on to someone else. When my set is finished, I collect my money, go backstage, put a robe on and go into the audience to talk with the customers. The rule is that they have to buy me drinks to keep me talking. I order champagne, but it's really ginger ale. They get expensive stuff, watered down."

"And that's all? They just buy you drinks?"

"Every so often I get a customer to buy a bottle of champagne, which goes for $300, and sit with me at a table in the back and talk. I make $30 for that. And sometimes they tip more."

"And all you ever do is talk?"

"You can't believe what these men will spend just to talk to me. I might even be more expensive than you are."

She said it with a sneer, lifting her head and looking down at me. I let the jab pass.

"Listen, they touch me, they're dead. The club has men who stop by my table every 10 minutes or so to make sure I'm okay. Nothing's ever happened. The club rules are,

'You can look, but you can't touch.' The owners don't want to get busted. But look, if I like the guy, we can always make a deal for later."

I wasn't sure what, if anything, to do about Mary. How much responsibility should a therapist take for a patient? I asked her if she used condoms and she told me she wasn't stupid. Mary wasn't doing anything immoral, certainly not by New York City standards. Then again, her actions could be damaging to Rebecca and others inside her. Some internal personalities said that as children they had been forced to dance before men. They were horrified that one of them was doing it again.

I once asked Mary what she thought about this. But she just told me how much she liked her work, especially having so much power over the men in the audience. Some were professionals, she said. She didn't care that she was causing an internal disturbance. She didn't even consider herself a member of the parliament and refused to abide by its decisions. It occurred to me as I listened to her that Mary's attitude might really be resistance in another form. Perhaps Rebecca had reached a plateau.

Rebecca had not talked much about her past since the initial burst of abreactions, I realized as I thought about the case. The memories had been bottled up inside her all during her previous therapy, she once told me, and now they had been cleared out. She was better now, she insisted. I knew there was more—maybe much more—to come. Perhaps this problem with Mary would be the way to get Rebecca's case moving again.

The pot reached full boil when Mary went out one night with a group of girls to "work" a private party. It was a disaster. Two men who were supposed to go along to protect them never showed up, and before the party ended Mary was forced to have sex with five men. This didn't seem to bother her much though. After all, she said, she was well paid for her trouble. But it raised havoc with other alters, who were painfully aware of what was happening. It took me weeks just to calm everybody down. Then I hypnotized Rebecca and asked to speak to a member of the Board. A personality named Sasha came out. She had the clipped diction, erect posture and commanding presence of a corporate executive. And, unlike Rebecca, she didn't fidget.

"I think what's happening with Mary might be dangerous for all of you," I told Sasha. "We've really got to come to some resolution about it. I need your help."

"We know. We've been concerned for a while. Mary's behavior is upsetting the children. They don't like being paid for displaying her body or for having sex. The feminist alters are irate. There has been some talk of killing Mary."

"But if they kill Mary, all of you will die."

"The Board knows that," she said crisply, "but some of the others think that they are separate entities. We've tried to reason with Mary, but as you know she won't even come to our meetings."

"Maybe I can help. But I need to know much more about Mary. Especially why she was created. I need to understand the reasons for her behavior."

"I'll have to consult with the other Board members. Excuse me please."

Her eyes closed and her chin dropped onto her chest. She was motionless for a few moments. Then she raised her head and reassumed Sasha's formal bearing.

"I have conferred with them. They do not think that you have a workable plan to help us, but given the seriousness of the situation and the fact that there is no better alternative, we are willing to talk to you."

Not exactly a vote of confidence, I thought to myself. I went ahead anyway.

"How and why was Mary created?"

"Why is easy," Sasha said. "She was created by the cult to perform at ceremonies and at other times."

"As simple as that?"

"Yes. They created a number of alters for various purposes. Mary was one of them."

"They purposely created alters?"

"Yes. They were fully aware of what you call multiple personality disorder, although they didn't call it that. They would create personalities for different functions. Mary was like a geisha. She would dance and take care of men."

Once the machinery for multiplicity is set up, new alters can be stamped out like widgets coming off an assembly line. But I had never heard of any group intentionally creating an alter in a person.

I thought back to Helen's attack. What I was thinking was unbelievable, but at the same time utterly logical. Could a cult—assuming of course that one existed—have created a personality inside Helen whose purpose was to attack anyone who came close to finding out about it? Could this cult have created an internal hit man, a Manchurian candidate, to protect its secrecy?

The cult was supposedly engaged in illegal activities, or so Rebecca said. If true, it would need to maintain the secrecy and loyalty of its members, as well as the silence of its victims. But there was always the risk that someone could become disaffected and try to betray it. Mere threats might not be enough. But what about an internal personality whose job was to maintain the cult's secrecy at all costs? This personality could inhibit its host from entering therapy, or disrupt a session if a person managed to seek out a therapist. Was that what happened with Helen?

As it turned out, the movie *The Manchurian Candidate* had been released on videotape and I had recently seen it for the first time in years. The protagonist, Raymond Shaw, had been captured by the Chinese communists during the Korean War and brainwashed in Manchuria. Once Shaw was back in the United States, the telephone would ring and a voice on the line would say, "Why don't you pass the time by playing a little solitaire?" Shaw would then find a deck of cards and start to play, stopping when he flipped over the Queen of Diamonds. Forty-five minutes later, the phone would ring again and the voice would ask, "Can you see the red queen?" Shaw would answer yes and then receive his instructions.

The Queen of Diamonds was a cue designed to access some part of Shaw—an alter personality?—trained by the Chinese to kill on command. Once accessed, this part could be given instructions. (He was supposed to kill a presidential candidate, but "snapped out of it" just in time.)

The Manchurian Candidate, though fiction, was loosely based on techniques used during that period. Could a cult have programmed Helen the same way the Chinese programmed Shaw? Could the cue have been my attempt to break through its secrecy? I wondered if that was what had happened to Ned. Could he have been programmed to kill himself upon a cue, such as the roses that were sent to him in the hospital? And if it could happen to Ned and Helen, why couldn't it happen to Rebecca? Was Mary simply an erotic entertainer, or did she have some other function? Understanding Mary might be the key not only to Rebecca, but also to Helen. And maybe even to Ned.

"Can you tell me how Mary was created?" I asked Sasha.

"I guess so. But it will take a few minutes for us to gather the data."

Sasha's eyes closed. The body slumped. After about two minutes, her eyes opened.

"I have it now. Are you ready?"

It wasn't so much a question as a command. I nodded.

"As usual, they woke her up in the middle of the night, put her in the cage and drove her to the farmhouse where they held their ceremonies. They put her in a tiny room. It was dark. She stayed there for a long time. We do not know how long. She had no food and no water. There was no place to go to the bathroom. She tried to hold it in, but couldn't. She had to sit in her own excrement."

She kept right on going with her narrative. There was no feeling, no change in expression, no affect. It was as if she were reading from an annual report.

"Then they came in. They gave her enemas. They said it

was to wash the good out of her so that the evil could be put in. They did it several times.

"After that, they left her alone again for a long time. Her mind started to drift. At first she told herself stories to pass the time. She drifted into a kind of fantasy land. She started to see things. Birds would fly around. They would talk to her, tell her stories. She got to know them. She gave them names."

It reminded me of times when I was young and had a high fever. I would lie in bed for I don't know how long, my mind just floating.

"After a while they took her into another room, where there were bright flashing lights. Strobes, I think they call them. And it had one of those mirrored balls hanging from the ceiling that spreads light around in swirls. They left her in her cage in the center of this room for a long time. There were five other cages, each containing a child. There was very little room in the cages. They had to sit on their haunches. They all looked terrified.

"Then the drums started to beat. Da-dummmm . . . da-dummmm . . . da-dummmm. Da-dummmm . . . da-dummmm . . . da-dummmm. Da-dummmm . . . da-dummmm . . . da-dummmm.

"They got louder and louder, then softer and softer. Fortunately, we weren't affected by it. We had left the body and floated up to the ceiling. We watched it all from above.

"Then the devils came out. They danced around her and started to chant. 'Hail Satan. Hail Satan.' Like that. To the same beat as the drums."

I almost hate to admit it now, but as I listened to her story I thought about New Year's Eve in 1969, when I was at Esalen Institute in Big Sur. The entertainment was a group of six drummers who literally came out of the hills and looked like they had lived there for years. They had long hair, shaggy beards and tattered jeans—the uniform of the nearly ended decade. They drummed and drummed all night, while we danced and danced. They didn't take a single break. Neither did we. At some point I went into some kind of state. My mind went blank. It was sensory overload.

I thought of Pavlov, the Russian physiologist best known for developing the concept of the conditioned response. He would ring a bell and give a dog some food. After a while he could just ring the bell to make the dog salivate. But Pavlov also discovered that putting a dog under extreme stress could erase the programming, washing its brain clean. He learned this in 1924, when a huge flood nearly drowned a group of dogs in his Leningrad laboratory. A worker saved them at the last moment, but Pavlov noticed that the previously conditioned responses had disappeared. Eventually, he found he could deprogram or brainwash the dogs using stressors such as electric shocks or by depriving them of food or simply by confusing them.

I was temporarily deprogrammed as I listened to the drumming that New Year's Eve at Esalen, and maybe Rebecca was, too, as she listened to the drumming in that farmhouse. From her description, it seemed possible that she was being brainwashed through sensory overload, and that, once her mind was blank, she would be receptive to programming.

I realized Sasha was still talking.

"They took one of the other girls out of the cage and told her to dance. She danced for a while. She wasn't very good. Her heart wasn't in it. They kept telling her to do better, but she couldn't. Maybe she was too frightened. After a while, they stopped her. They said she didn't dance good enough. And they put her on the altar and killed her."

Sasha didn't say how they killed her, and I didn't ask. I have learned that if I ask too many questions of these patients, they begin to think I don't believe them. And in this case, I didn't, but I didn't want her to know that.

"They then went to the next cage and took another girl out. They told her to dance, and she did. She was better than the first. They liked her. They appeared to get aroused.

And then all the devils had sex with her, while she cried. But that got them mad. They put her in a box with the girl that they had just killed."

"Where were you during all this?"

"We were still on the ceiling, watching."

"We?"

"Yes. The Board. We were away from it, so we didn't feel anything. But it was bad for her. She was frightened. She was confused."

"Then what happened?"

"A devil took her out of the cage. He placed his hands on her shoulders, looked into her eyes and said, 'You are Satan's child. You will serve Satan. You will receive a great reward from the Lord of Lords for performing well.'

"At that point Mary was created. She knew just what to do. She said, 'Yes, Lord. I am Satan's daughter. I know what to do. I will do it.' "

"How did Mary know what to do?"

"Someone had to save us. We had been through this before. We had been in the cages before, watching, like the other two girls.

"Mary got up and started to dance to the drums. One by one she went over to each man and danced close to him and ran her hand up his leg. It got more and more frantic. Then the men took her and placed her on the altar and had sex with her.

"When it was over, they took her to this platform and sat her down on it. I guess it was sort of like a throne. And all the people in the room cheered. They told her that from now on she would teach the others. She would not have to endure any more pain. Then they all sat down to a huge feast."

This was more than Pavlov put his dogs through, of course, but the method seemed similar. Create a sensory overload that washes out all previous programming, which in this case, perhaps, was normal behavior. Tell them what you want to do and show them the punishment if they don't comply. Then reward them afterward, to reinforce the pattern. Pair pain with pleasure, to the beating of drums. Was she another Manchurian candidate, trained not to kill, but to dance, to arouse, to stimulate? It was farfetched, but there was a logic to it. A crazy logic.

If I was going to stop Mary from dancing and keep Rebecca out of the sex halls, I realized I was going to have to abreact the memory of her creation. But more than that, I would have to have all the alters who experienced it abreact it. Like a diamond that has been shattered, the trauma was dissociated into many parts. According to the theory, the experience must come out the way it goes in.

The trouble was, I wasn't sure how many alters had been invested with the memory. And, of course, the uncooperative Mary would have to play a role in the abreaction, too. Only by watching her own creation would she finally believe that she was part of Rebecca, not a separate entity. Only when she accepted that she was part of the group would she change her mind about dancing.

"We can't handle the pain," Sasha said when I told her what I had in mind for Rebecca and all the others.

"I know. But we have to try. If it looks like anyone is having trouble, we can send them into the back room we used before."

She had an apprehensive expression as she reached up and touched the amber stone that hung around her neck. I must say I didn't blame her.

"Look, why don't you put all the children in the back room now. Let's only have Mary and those who participated in the ritual go through it again. I'll free up a time later in the week when we can have a longer session. We'll try to go through it then."

ON the appointed day Rebecca arrived precisely on time, her red hair hidden under a pale-green scarf that protected it from the mists of the chilly evening. I asked her to lie on the couch, and I was able to put her into a trance simply by counting down from 20. That seemed like a good sign. I asked to speak to Mary, and when she came out I asked if she had heard us talking about her at the last session. She said she had listened for awhile but grew bored and went away. I told her we were going to take another look at the memory of that ritual and asked her to stay around to watch. Reluctantly, she agreed. Or at least she nodded.

And then I prepared to go through it again. The children, the murder, the dancing, the rape. I brought out Sasha and asked her who the little girl in the cage was.

"Would you like to meet her?"

"You read my mind."

Her change in posture left no doubt there was a switch.

"Who are you?" I asked.

"Becky. I'm the one that goes in the cage, since I'm the smallest and it doesn't hurt me as much."

She sounded like a child, much younger than Mary.

"Did you dance, too?"

"Noooo. Too scared."

"What did you do?"

"My job was to stay in the cage. I have been doing it since I was little. I am best for it, because I am small."

"Okay, I want you to remember that night in the cage."

At that moment, she started to shake. I could imagine a terrified child, trying not to urinate or defecate, squatting there while the strobes played and drums beat, seeing the first girl killed and watching the second one raped.

Then Becky started to scream. There was hardly any noise coming out of her mouth, but the veins on her forehead stood out. I thought they would burst. I sat next to her and at her request held her hand as I watched her remember. I don't ordinarily touch a patient, but this abreaction was so intense, and Rebecca looked so young and frightened, I felt that some contact was necessary. I was even tempted to rescue her, to move the memory more quickly, to get it over with. But I knew it would be more for my needs than my patient's.

At this point, Becky told me that she was taken from the cage and Mary was somehow born. And within a few moments, Becky became Mary. Or at least I assumed it was Mary, because she got off the couch and began an erotic dance in my office, gyrating her hips. Then she lay on the couch and apparently relived the rape that came after her dance in the memory. Then it stopped, and she lay there, exhausted.

I had seen enough for one day.

"Mary? Are you all right?"

"I guess so."

"You know, you took the pain and saved everybody. It was a bad thing they did to you. They forced you to have sex. You might think you enjoyed it, but many parts of you didn't like it at all."

"What do you mean?"

"Listen inside your head for a minute as I ask a question. 'Did all of you inside like it? Tell Mary what it was like.'"

After a few seconds, she began to squirm.

"They are all the parts of you that you protected by pretending to enjoy what they did to you. And they are telling you that when you dance now they are in pain. It reminds them of this experience, this terrible experience."

"I feel tired," Mary said. "I need to think."

I realized that she was trying to break off the session. It must have been too much for her to absorb. I hoped that I had at least managed to make her feel more like a member of the group, and perhaps to realize that her behavior was causing her "siblings" pain.

"All right, Mary, close your eyes. As I count down from twenty you will drift into a nice sleep. I want you to lie down and take a nice, peaceful, long nap, while you think about what you recalled here today. We will talk again next time."

She was relaxed at last. I waited a few minutes.

"Okay, when I count to five, Rebecca will be back in charge of the body. She can take all these memories back, with all the feelings that she is able to handle. One. Two. Three. Four. Five. Eyes open. Wide awake."

Rebecca looked around the room and recognized where she was. Then she just sat there, silent and dazed, for a few minutes. When she spoke, she was angry.

"Those bastards," she said, clenching her ringed hands. "They used me when I was a child, when I was a teenager. They used me until I went away to school. I even think he did it when I was at college, but I'm not sure.

"My father would come over to me. He always scared me. He was a big man. He had these huge hands. He would place them on my arms just below my shoulders. He would stare into my eyes and say, 'I want you to dance for the men.' He would make me go to parties and I would dance. Then I would go to bed with some of the men. Sometimes they gave me money to take back to my father. All those times. All those times. That son of a bitch. I'm glad he's dead, because I would kill him now if I could."

"You don't have to do that anymore," I said. "Those days are gone. They are over."

She looked at me for a moment. Then she looked away and began to cry. I could feel her sadness across the room.

Chapter 10

THE EVIL ONE

I found myself thinking about *The Manchurian Candidate* in the days and weeks after Helen attacked me. Particularly about how Major Bennett Marco was able to deprogram Raymond Shaw. Marco had discovered that the device used to cue Shaw was the Queen of Diamonds. Like a Las Vegas dealer, he fanned out a deck of 52 queens, all diamonds. Then, looking at Shaw, Marco said his magic was stronger than theirs. And that was how he canceled the programming.

It was good theater, but not much help to me with Helen. Yes, what is learned can be unlearned. But if Helen had been abused by a cult, the programming was likely to be complicated and multilayered, having been built up over years. And I was hardly an expert in this area. To attempt a systematic deprogramming, like those performed by professionals hired to reclaim people from religious cults, was beyond me. It was a job for a behavioral psychologist, not an analyst.

But I did have the tools of psychotherapy. And I had a patient who I believed was ready to cooperate, despite the startling attack. Some part of Helen was stronger than the programming. I was convinced of it. I had to find that part, even if it meant tiptoeing through a mine field. I had easily parried Helen's lunge. If I had to, I could do it again. So I resolved to move forward, although cautiously. The first step was to see how much support I could count on from my patient.

"Do you remember a few weeks ago, after that incident where you found your clothes in a different locker in the health club?" I asked Helen at our next session. "You agreed to be hypnotized to find out what had happened, remember?"

"Strange, wasn't it," she said uncertainly. She was biting her nails, one by one. It was a new habit that didn't go well with her professional attire. "I do that type of thing a lot. Misplace things, I mean. It's been that way since I was a child."

She would have moved into one of her extended, self-critical monologues had I not cut her off.

"Helen, we have a problem here that I want to talk to you about. It's important that we find out about your past, but there are parts of you that seem to believe it would be dangerous."

"What are you talking about?"

I could almost hear the ice cracking under my feet, but I decided to keep going. I couldn't help but notice, with relief, that Helen had left her purse on the couch, three feet from her chair—it might contain a weapon—and that her dress did not have any pockets in which armaments might be hidden. I was thankful as well that I had "patient proofed" my office after her attack, removing any sharp objects that might have been within her reach now. I even got rid of a vase of flowers that I sometimes kept near the bentwood chair and a pair of heavy brass bookends shaped like sailboats. And I had taken the added precaution of keeping a small can of hair spray where I could instantly reach it. Someone once told me that, sprayed in the face, it would act like mace—which is illegal in New York City—and temporarily disarm an attacker. Some colleagues have gone much farther. A psychiatrist in Philadelphia told me he had installed a tear-gas canister in the walls of his office, along with closed-circuit television. He also had a stun gun at his side. Others outfitted their offices with panic buttons. Perhaps it was arrogance—or just the fact that Helen, though a large woman, was much smaller than I—but I had faith in our therapeutic relationship.

"The last time we tried to talk about this, Helen, one of your personalities came out and lunged at me," I reminded her. "We had a bit of a tussle. I haven't brought it up until now because I didn't know how we could work with it. But now I do. Do you remember anything about it?"

She had a puzzled expression, but the nail-biting had stopped.

"I remember something like that, but I thought it was just one of those dreams I have. Are you all right, Dr. Mayer? Did I hurt you? I would feel terrible if I did anything to harm you. I know how much you have to put up with."

She was trying to change the subject again. Rather than call her attention to this resistance, I bypassed it by thanking her for her concern and assuring her that no damage had been done. I did tell her that we needed to prevent a recurrence. Helen asked what she could do.

"I think that we have to work hypnotically to find out who inside you wants to prevent the information I asked you about from getting out, and why. And it would be good to know if that individual has any allies in there."

She thought for a moment.

"This all sounds like a movie. But whatever you want to do is all right with me."

I was able to put Helen into a trance, a positive sign. Still, I decided to take an additional precaution. I gave her a post-hypnotic suggestion that she was to go into a deeper trance immediately if I said the word "close," a word I always used in inductions when I would instruct patients to close their eyes.

I tried out the command a few times and it worked. Helen would get a glazed look at the sound of the word. I wasn't sure I would get the same results in a time of real need, but that's why I had the hair spray nearby.

"Can I talk to the person who I talked to a while back, the person who warned me about the Evil One?" I said, gingerly beginning the exploration.

I didn't really expect an answer, not a verbal one anyway. I suspected I would have to have her write it out, like before. So I was taken aback when the body before me stiffened and a voice much harsher than Helen's curtly replied, "What do you want?"

"Thank you for talking to me," I said, trying to maintain my balance. "We need some help. I suppose that you are aware of what happened the last time. I was talking to you and some other part came out and attacked me."

"Yes. We told you to beware of the Evil One. You were arrogant. You didn't listen. And I'm not sure you're listening now. Why are you pursuing this?"

"You're right. I should have listened. Please stop me if I start asking questions that will upset anyone. I'm just trying to help all of you. I'm sure that you are just trying to protect me, as the other one was doing his or her job protecting Helen. I'm also impressed at what a fine job he or she did. I was scared. But is there any way that I could talk to that other one, so that I can tell it what a fine job it is doing to protect Helen?"

"Are you crazy? Don't you remember what happened?"

"But I have a better understanding of all that now. I know that whoever that personality is, he or she must protect Helen. I know that if any information gets out, Helen's life might be in danger. When I asked about the cult, I had to be attacked. I understand that now. Look at how cautious I am. How careful I am. Look how long it took me to bring it up again."

My approach was designed to get under the Evil One's defenses by accepting rather than attacking its reasoning. Attacking resistance only strengthens it.

"I wonder if I can talk to that part of Helen now. But before I do, you know I feel funny referring to such an important person so impersonally. Is it male or female? Does it have a name?"

"She doesn't want to tell you her name. She wants you to go away."

Giving someone your name makes some people, children especially, feel like they are giving up some of their power. But now at least I knew the Evil One was female. And I was communicating with her, albeit through an intermediary. Encouraged, I pressed forward.

"What about you? You can tell me your name, can't you?"

"They call me Claire. I'm able to see a lot of what goes on and what has gone on."

Claire, I reasoned, was shorthand for clairvoyant. The names multiples give their alters are sometimes strangely clever. Then again, sometimes they are just plain childish. And sometimes alters are simply and bluntly named after a characteristic or an emotion they represent. Patients usually aren't very consistent about these names. Helen had alters named Meg and Alice, but also a personality menacingly known as the Evil One. And Rebecca had an eclectic bunch, too—Arlene, Becky and Mary; Sasha and the Board of Directors; Artonoxima, the priestess initiate, and Obedience.

Claire told me that she had been watching me and knew I was trying to help. I explained that I was attempting to understand, and perhaps undo, Helen's programming. Claire became silent and seemed to withdraw. I interpreted this as an indication that I was on the right track.

"Claire, you know we had a problem here a while back."

"Well, we warned you."

"Yes, I know. I approached certain subjects that I suppose I should not have."

"Yes." She nodded and her dark brown hair swung back and forth.

"It seems to me that no one really wanted to hurt me." She didn't respond.

"Let me talk to you very clearly. I think it's important that we understand what caused the attack and try to find ways to keep it from happening again. Someone must have done something to the so-called Evil One to make her react that way. I think we have to find out what happened."

She nodded.

"I assume by your response that it was done by bad people."

Another slight nod.

"People that hurt children?"

Again, a nod.

"And I suppose that if the secret gets out, it will be very bad for you?"

Her eyes dropped.

"Tell me what is going on."

Finally, she spoke.

"I can't tell you, because if I do, if any of us do, the Evil One will kill us." Her olive skin flushed darker. "She is responsible for keeping us quiet. I can tell you that, but I can't tell you what we have to be quiet about. That's all that I can safely say."

The session was almost over. I used the remaining minutes to bring Helen out of her trance and get a commitment for further hypnotic work at our next session. She looked dazed, which often happens after an intense hypnotic session. It's almost like switching time zones. I sometimes wonder what my doorman thinks as he helps these patients into cabs.

I didn't get very far into the mine field, but at least I had come back alive.

No one was going to tell me about Helen's programming for fear of the Evil One. My only option was to talk to the Evil One herself.

My luck. I needed the cooperation of the one part of Helen whose job it was to be uncooperative.

I thought about immobilizing Helen—with her permission, of course—while I tried to conduct the interview. At least I wouldn't have to worry about another attack. But I feared that might make a permanent enemy out of the Evil One. No, I would have to confront her without benefit of restraints. Somehow, I needed to build a relationship with her even though she was programmed to resist.

When Helen arrived for her next session, I put her into a trance simply by telling her to "close" her eyes. I was relieved that the word still worked. I asked to speak to Claire and after a few moments of small talk asked her to check on the Evil One.

Claire paused for a moment, as if she were talking to someone inside. Then she returned and told me that the Evil One didn't understand why I kept bothering her.

"Tell her that I would like to meet her," I said. "Tell her that I promise not to talk about the things that I am not supposed to talk about."

She responded with a sheepish look.

"She wants to come out and tear your head off. Or slit you up the center and watch you bleed to death. She says she is going to eat your heart."

She looked at me apologetically. Then she started to bite the nails on her left hand.

"Sorry, but that's what she told me to say."

"Tell her I'm impressed. And tell her that if she comes

out I won't talk about things she doesn't want to talk about. But she has to agree not to harm me or anything in this office."

I was offering her a chance to face her adversary, and perhaps be understood. For all her bravado, I was betting the opportunity would appeal to her. Anyway, if I've learned one thing about multiples, it's that they love drama. (So, perhaps, do their therapists.)

"She says she'll talk to you," Claire said. "But you're going to be sorry. She says that she doesn't need to be violent. She can cut deeper with words than with a knife."

"Thank her for the warning."

Before I was quite ready, Helen's eyes flashed and her lips tightened into red lines that no longer quite covered her clenched teeth.

"Remember what happened last time," she hissed. It was not phrased as a question.

"Don't worry. It's impressed on my memory. You certainly are effective at protecting the group."

"I'm not taking care of anyone."

"I thought your job was to protect everyone."

"What makes you think I protect them?"

"Well, the last time we met, I was asking the wrong questions and you attacked me. I assumed you did it to prevent the information from getting out, because if it got out somebody would be hurt."

She sat there and glared. Then she said, "I didn't like your attitude. Why should I waste my time talking to you? Your chest might be hard to cut through, but I know right where to put the knife, and I'm strong enough to reach in and pull your heart out while it is still beating." The cords in her neck stood out and Helen's man-tailored, navy blue suit seemed hardly able to contain this new angry persona.

I was ready to yell "close" or to grab for the hair spray if she even slightly moved toward me. But some part of me was also calm. After all, the Evil One had agreed to talk to me.

"I'm sure you're very good at what you do." I waited a few moments for effect. "You must love them very much to risk your job to protect them."

"I don't love anyone. I just do my job."

"I'm sorry. I was just curious about your job. I wonder whether you really like it."

"I love my job."

"I think it might be a tough job."

"What do you mean?"

"Well, you have to put your life on the line to protect them. And just who are you protecting?"

She didn't answer.

"Are you sure you don't love anyone? I think you are really very noble to protect the others."

"I don't feel anything. I just do my job."

"Are you sure? I wonder if there is some part of you that thinks it got the short end by always having to be the tough one."

"Not a chance."

"I wonder. Look, we've gone this far. Indulge me. Let's have everyone go away for a few minutes. Then you can let me know how you really feel. If some part of you thinks you are always doing the tough job, wiggle one of your fingers."

While she glared at me, the index finger of her right hand trembled. I stared at the finger until she looked at it, too. But I didn't say anything. I didn't want to humiliate her.

"You must be very lonely because of your job."

"I'm not lonely. I don't know where you got that idea. You know, you're really annoying me. And I can get very vicious when I'm annoyed."

As she said that, her index finger moved again. She saw it, too.

"I think I could show you some things that might change your mind," I said. "All you have to do is promise not to attack me while I ask Claire some questions. You can listen to the answers and then we can talk. What do you say? Look, you can always kill me later," I added reasonably.

She sat there for a moment. Then she was gone and Claire returned. Helen's body seemed to deflate to its normal proportions.

"You seem to know a lot about what happened, Claire, but have been afraid to tell me. Do you know how and when the Evil One came into being? I think it's safe to tell me now."

"Are you sure it's safe?"

"This is very important, Claire. It's the only way you can get free of this. Sometimes, all of us have to take a chance. Playing it safe leaves us stuck."

For a while she was silent. Then she raised her eyes toward mine, and she began to speak.

"We were brought to a place we had been many times. We were in a room, a dark room, for a long time. I don't know how long. Then someone came in and brought us to another room. There were people with their faces covered. There were children there, too.

"They took us out and placed us on a table. They rubbed some lotion on parts of our body and put cold metal things over them. There were wires that ran to a box a man held. They put it on her face, by her cheeks, on her palms and between her legs."

I was sure she had switched to the third person as a defense.

"Then they started to ask her questions. They asked her if she knew any of the people. She said 'Yes, that looks like my Daddy.' And then her body jumped."

I winced, remembering times when I had accidentally received an electrical shock. I asked Claire if she felt it. She said she did not feel anything. I was sorry to have broken the narrative, and asked her to go on.

"They asked her again if she recognized anyone. She said, 'Some of Daddy's friends.' Then her body twitched again.

"They accused her of telling secrets. She said she didn't, and she got another shock. They accused her of making friends at school. She denied it, and there was another shock. It seemed like any answer was wrong. If she said yes, they shocked her. If she said no, they shocked her. Then they made her repeat their words.

" 'If you talk to anyone, we will know, and we will get you,' they said.

" 'You are a child of Satan and must remain silent.'

" 'You are one of us.'

" 'Only we understand you.'

" 'Only we love you.'

" 'Those on the outside do not love you.'

" 'Those on the outside will hurt you.'

" 'You must remain silent.'

At that point, Claire told me, the Evil One took over the body.

" 'I will do anything you want,' she told the men. 'I will never tell. I will make sure that no one tells. I swear on my life.' "

"What happened next?"

"They took the electrodes off."

"And then?"

"The leader told her they would always take care of her. That she was a part of them. Then they brought this young girl out. She was naked and trying to cover herself with her hands. She was brought in front of the group. The leader said, 'You have told secrets to an outsider. We have told you time and time again that we are your friends and they are your enemies. You have chosen not to listen. We will make an example of you.'

"Two other men grabbed her arms and held her down while the leader came over and picked up a knife."

Claire paused, looked straight into my eyes and said, "He killed her."

It may not have been true, any of it, but her body was reacting as if there were no doubt of its veracity. As for me, I felt nauseous and dizzy. Claire continued.

" 'This body is impure,' the leader said. 'We will consign it to the flames.'

"We all went outside and stood in the middle of a field. He poured something over the girl, handed me a burning torch and made her set her on fire."

"Who set her on fire?" I asked Claire. "The Evil One?"

"No. She went away. The Fire Lady came out and did it. The smell was horrible.

"After that they brought over a bowl that had eyeballs in it. They made us eat one. It popped like a grape when she bit down on it. They told us that now they had eyes inside of us that could see whatever we were doing.

"Then they gave her something sweet to eat. She got very drowsy. Everything was foggy. She went to sleep.

"When she woke up, there was a cut on her stomach, with stitches. She cried, because it hurt.

"The leader told us that they had planted a bomb inside of us that would go off if we told anyone about what happened."

With that, Helen pulled her blouse out of her skirt and showed me a very faint scar on her right side, near her waist.

"A man came over and raped her. She switched into Scarlett. Scarlett takes the rapes. When he was done, he said, 'You are consecrated. Satan is now inside you. He will go wherever you go. You cannot escape him.'

"They sent her back to the first room. She found her clothes and put them on. Then her mother came in. Her mother didn't seem to care about how she looked. She took her hand and led her to the car and drove home."

It was similar to what Rebecca said she went through, a primitive but powerful programming. The initial trauma would have forced a dissociation. Then they reinforced the dissociated state with praise and group acceptance. They made her think that they could watch her all the time. They bonded her to the group by making her believe she took part in a killing. Then, like a marriage, they consummated the union with a sexual act. And as a final twist of the knife, her mother pretended not to have been a part of it and ignored the event, acting as if it never happened and giving her a model of how to act after such episodes.

Perhaps because I was so horrified at its content, I only now realized that Claire had told me her story practically without emotion. I was going to have to abreact it with her someday. I did not look forward to that.

I asked to speak to the Evil One again.

"Well, did you hear all that?" I asked her after the switch.

She wasn't hissing anymore. She looked shaken, even frightened.

"Now you know," she said softly. "Now you know that they will kill us."

"Well, you didn't blow up," I argued.

She didn't respond. She just rubbed her lips with her index finger.

"They programmed you." I said. "They needed secrecy. They created you to ensure that."

"It's all over. They will kill them. I have failed to do my job. I have to kill myself."

"Nonsense," I said, reminding her that Helen's parents were both dead. "They can't hurt you anymore. You know they are dead."

"Yes, but it doesn't feel like they are dead."

She stared straight at me. Her fearful expression told me that for her they were very much alive.

I took another route. "I don't think there is a bomb. I think they did that to scare you. You didn't explode, did you?"

She looked down at her midsection.

"Maybe it will happen later," she said apprehensively.

"Will you hold off doing anything long enough for us to have a doctor examine you and take an X ray?" As I said that, I had a better idea. "Maybe someone has already examined you," I thought out loud.

I quickly brought Claire out and she said that years ago Helen had gone to a doctor for a stomach ailment and he had performed an upper and lower gastro-intestinal series. I might have suspected as much. Many of my patients have physical problems at one time or another. Rebecca constantly suffered from chest pains and intestinal cramps.

"You mean they just tried to frighten me?" the Evil One said after she had taken control of the body again.

"Exactly."

"What about the rest of us? I have to protect them. They'll kill us."

"Your parents are dead. They can't hurt you anymore," I told her.

"But they are always watching me. Sometimes they send me letters. Sometimes I think I see them on the street, following me."

"I can understand how frightened you are, but I think I have a way that will help you protect yourself. You can write down the names of everybody you saw at the rituals and send them to a lawyer, with instructions to make them public if anything happens to you. Then you make sure everyone knows what you've done."

If there was a cult—if any of this was true—the last thing a member would want to do is attract attention. This list might be a powerful deterrent. Some patients have gone to amazing lengths, depositing many lists with many people. Anyway, what was the harm? Even if all that I had just heard was a paranoid delusion, such an action might make Helen feel a little more secure.

"I can't believe that they did all those horrible things to us," she said after a while. "And, by the way, my name isn't really The Evil One. It's Martha."

Chapter 11

THE
CONFERENCE

IT was the last day of the International Conference for the Study of Multiple Personality and Dissociation in Chicago. I had given a talk on the history of Satanism and it had gone well. The October weather was perfect. I was staying in a luxurious hotel.

And to my amazement, my patients back home were quiet. Usually, whenever I go away at least one of them will have a problem, and I find myself interrupting my time off with phone call after phone call. Given the intensity of the episodes my patients and I had been through, I had been expecting to hear from one of them at least once or twice. But I didn't.

In Chicago, I was with my tribe—600 colleagues who believed, as I do, that multiple personality disorder is far more prevalent than once thought. In the hotel meeting rooms, at least, the diagnosis had finally attained respectability.

How much things had changed since I began treating Toby, my first multiple. Back then there was scarcely anyone to talk to about her. Now there are hundreds, maybe thousands, of therapists treating patients with multiple personality disorder. And from what I had learned at the conference, some had patients who, like Ned, Rebecca and Helen, may have been victims of ritual abuse.

For example, one of the conference participants, a psychiatrist at an in-patient unit specializing in dissociative and related disorders, talked about patients who had been trained by cults to respond to threatening situations in ways that would protect the groups. Like me, he had even been attacked by a patient. The patient had given him a tape recorder and asked him to tape the session. At the patient's request, he checked the tape to make sure it was blank. When he turned on the machine some music played, apparently triggering the incident.

I found some reassurance in a paper presented by George Greaves, "A Cognitive-Behavioral Approach to the Treatment of MPD Ritually Abused Satanic Cult Survivors." Dr. Greaves, a psychologist who was the founder of the International Society for the Study of Multiple Personality and Dissociation, argued that the fact that patients have been programmed to respond in a certain way made them better candidates for treatment "precisely because they have been systematically conditioned." "Such systematic conditioning makes possible a structured plan for deconditioning," he concluded. What can be conditioned can be deconditioned.

One of the final events of the conference was a daylong seminar on ritual abuse. Such sessions had been held for several years, as the profession struggled to come to terms with increasing reports of these episodes. But this was the first one I had attended. I didn't know what to expect, but I hoped that I would come away with some new tools to help me back in New York.

Container of tea in hand, I took my seat. On the podium were a half dozen people, most of whom identified themselves as survivors of cults.*

THE first to move to the microphone was a woman named Janet. Her motivation, like that of the others at the session, seemed clear to me. She was speaking out now to help therapists who seemed to be encountering more and more patients like her. And she was also sending a message of encouragement directly to those who believed they had been victims of ritual abuse.

Before she began, Janet warned us that her talk would be graphic and gave us 30 seconds to ground ourselves in preparation. I would be glad she took this precaution.

In a remarkably clear voice and an almost matter-of-fact tone, Janet asserted that the abuse she had endured began when she was just a month or two old. She talked of a satanic group and spoke of its many horrifying acts, including, she said, the sacrifice of children.

She described what seemed like some sort of an initiation ceremony. It took place, she said, at an empty factory. There were people wearing masks and black robes. That reminded me of the stories I had heard from Ned and Rebecca. Janet recalled being spun around under psychedelic lights, apparently to disorient her. Her body was painted. She said she was being tested to see how much torture she could tolerate.

I sat there listening to Janet and not really knowing what to think. Sometimes, she said, the tortures were performed

* Since no transcript is available of the Chicago meeting, this chapter is based on recordings from a similar conference in Colorado at which some of the same people participated. Names and other details have been changed.

in rooms that were dark. Sometimes she endured abuse in
rooms dimly lit by candles. And what abuse. The episodes
she described chilled me. Janet spoke of being whipped by
the members of this horrible group, of being hung upside
down for extended periods. They spit on her. They threw
hot and cold water on her. They threw rocks, darts and even
knives at her, she said. Janet recalled being locked in
closets, above bees and snakes.

Symbols were branded onto her, she said, with hot irons.
She was convinced that her blood was taken and used in the
group's rituals. They applied leeches to her, she said. And
she said she was forced to chant repeatedly that she was a
child of Satan—and that she would always follow evil.

As I listened to Janet, my mind drifted back to the stories
I had heard in my office, from my own patients.

Just when she was being readied for what she thought
was some sort of sacrificial rite, Janet said, the police staged
a raid. The leaders of the group apparently got away, she
said, through what she described as a secret exit. Janet
recalled being taken to a hospital, only to be snatched back
by a member of the group. But the leaders had gone, she
went on, and she believed the group disbanded.

That was the end of her satanic abuse, she said. But Janet
said that she was subjected to incest until she went away to
college. She said she now had no contact with her father
and very little with her mother and brothers, who write to
her only at a post office box.

At this point Janet gave us another 30-second break,
which I needed. I realized that some part of me wanted to
doubt her stories. Was it simply that I didn't want to believe
I lived in a world where such things could happen?

But why, I kept asking myself, would anyone make up
such stories?

When Janet resumed speaking, she described her difficulties in trying to recover and heal herself. After being
locked in a dark basement, where she said people would
appear and disappear and fires would seem to start sponta-

neously, Janet no longer trusted her perceptions. Who could blame her, given what she said she had been through? She had to play with wooden blocks, she said, as a way of relearning reality.

To hear her tell it, the members of my profession did not seem very sympathetic or helpful, at least at first. Janet said she had seen many therapists before she finally found one who she thought could help her undo the brainwashing to which she said she had been subjected.

During her therapy, memories of the abuse she believed she suffered came back, but only in fragments. They had to be pieced together into a coherent narrative. Janet said she was afraid she would forever be evil, a feeling she learned to dissipate through holding her own cleansing rituals that were designed to cancel the original satanic rites. She staged her own ceremonies paying homage to other victims, including children she said she had seen killed. Once, she said, she made a small pillow of lace and silk as a remembrance of her own sister, who she said had been battered to death. It enabled her to put some sort of closure on the pain. And she learned to work around triggers, such as the sound of drums or certain dates on which rituals had occurred.

Despite all that Janet said she had been through—despite all that she related to us at the conference—she did not sound bitter. There was a sadness; that was certain. But her resolve and her strength also came through. That amazed me.

JANET finished her talk and made her way back to her seat. The silence in the room was broken only by an announcement that there would be a 15-minute break.

It was the last day of the conference. I had sat through more sessions than I cared to remember. There were discussions on the theory of dissociation, on hypnotic techniques, on understanding and coping with counter transference, which is what we therapists call our emotional reactions to our patients. So much sitting would normally have been enough to send my back into spasms of pain. And yet, as I listened to Janet, I found that I was completely absorbed.

I got up from my chair and joined the crowd at the coffee urns, looking around for a familiar face. I needed someone to talk to, someone with whom I could compare experiences. I wanted to know what my colleagues thought about Janet's presentation.

They were standing around in knots of twos and threes, talking. I didn't see anyone I knew, so I just wandered from group to group, overhearing bits and pieces of conversations. Some therapists were clearly in shock. I lingered on the edge of one group long enough to hear someone tell a story that gave me a chill. A young girl was sexually abused by a group of people who then brought out a live rabbit and told her to draw a picture of it, which she did. Then one of the adults held the rabbit in front of the child and stabbed it with a knife. The child was warned that if she told anyone about what they had done to her, what happened to the rabbit would happen to her. But that wasn't all. Three men in the group were dressed as a policeman, a judge and a doctor, the point apparently being that if she even thought of telling she would realize that there would be no help from doctors, judges or the police. And in a final, horrible twist, the man dressed as the policeman told the child to take the picture she had drawn home and tape it to the refrigerator door, where it would be a constant reminder of her ordeal and the penalty for revealing it.

And this was supposed to be a break from stress of the survivors' presentations, I thought to myself as I headed back to my seat.

NEXT was Dora. Like Janet, she spoke very crisply, in a voice that at times was nearly devoid of emotion, making her story seem all the more fantastic.

Dora, too, said her abuse had started when she was born. She said she had been raped and forced into prostitution when she was still quite young.

Dora said her victimizers had used a strategy that linked pleasurable situations with painful and sadistic ones. She spoke of being masturbated, for example, while being made to watch as an animal was somehow tortured. She said that when she was young, she would dutifully be taken to church, where she would hear all about the goodness of religion. But at other times she would be abused and compelled to take part in strange ceremonies. Sometimes, she said, she was placed in coffins.

It sounded as though Dora had been enshrouded throughout her childhood in a fog of confusion, secrecy, treachery and pain. She did not know basic facts about her family, such as the ages of her parents or the names of some relatives.

She was trained, she said, not to tell anyone what was happening to her or she would risk an even worse fate. Given what she said she had witnessed and what she said she had suffered, it seemed like a powerful threat.

And there was one more reason why she would be disinclined to tell, she said. She was afraid that if she did, whoever heard her horrifying tales would accuse her of being part of it all, of being a victimizer as well as a victim.

She stopped talking for a moment and let out a sob, or something that sounded like one. Much of what she had been saying so far reminded me of what I had heard in my office, especially when she discussed the combining of pleasure and pain. Many incest victims experience this duality. Take the father who rapes his daughter and then buys her an expensive gift and professes his love. But the pairing of pleasure and pain seemed to be especially common among the sort of groups my patients had described. Some of these groups seemed to have thought it out very carefully, using this combination in an insidious effort to turn a victim into a sadomasochist, someone who enjoys pain. But clearly, the technique didn't always work.

It was amazing, Dora continued, that she had been able to get away. I certainly had to agree. For years, she said, the only safe place for her was inside, by which I assumed she meant an internal world populated with alter personalities to help her. It was apparently some of those personalities who enabled her to make the break and escape.

But she also said that the very multiplicity that shielded her and helped free her also sabotaged her when she tried to live a normal life. She lost time and suffered swings of emotion for which she could not account. She couldn't control the actions of her alters. Some would not let her go to her therapy sessions. Some were still so repelled by her experiences as a child prostitute that they would throw away any money she had. Younger alters would take over the body at lunchtime and not let her go back to work.

Dora solved these problems by drawing up a series of ingenious contracts with her alters. There were agreements that enabled her to work, go to therapy, even fall asleep. (Some of the youngest alters were terrified to go to sleep, since Dora said most of her abuse occurred at night.) Eventually, she didn't need the contracts anymore, because through therapy and integration her life developed a structure that was strong enough to hold her together without any artificial internal supports.

Still, it made me think about some of the resistance I had been encountering from my patients. What I assumed was malicious and downright childish behavior might have been due to conflicts in my patients' internal worlds.

Dora talked about how much she tested her therapist with demands for more and more time, with rages, with childlike states and jealously. Some of her personalities did not regard her therapist as an ally, she said. In fact, they thought of her therapist more as a potential abuser, since the sessions were triggering intense and painful memories.

I would do well to have my patients turn out like Dora, I

thought to myself as I listened to her. She seemed to have broken through and severed the horrible bonds. Like Janet, Dora appeared to have accepted what she believed had happened to her and was now combating it with strength and resourcefulness.

She said she was integrated. But even more than that, she said she had come to be proud of her alter personalities, who had helped her and, in a way, saved her.

She wasn't seeking revenge. She was only seeking health, mental health. And, it seemed to me, she had attained it.

Her attitude reminded me of a story I once heard about a man who was liberated from a concentration camp. As he was limping across a bridge, he came across one of his old guards lying there wounded. He looked at him, debating with himself whether to throw him off. Then he simply stepped over the guard and continued his journey home.

THERE were other speakers at the session. I don't recall exactly how many. One of those identified as a survivor said she had been subjected to some sort of experimental surgery. Her doctor was amazed at how well she could get around now, she indicated, given what her X rays apparently revealed. Several therapists also spoke at the session, sharing their experiences in treating ritually abused patients.

After a while, the stories began to blur. I had heard about astonishing abuse and unimaginable horrors. And to make it even more remarkable, the incidents were often related in unemotional tones, with clinical precision. It was one thing to watch Ned, Rebecca and Helen abreact their episodes in my office. Now I was hearing others recalling remarkably similar events—others who appeared to be further along or even finished with their therapy. Were the stories true? How could they be? Could there really be such evil in the world? How could anyone survive it?

Early in his career, Freud confronted a disorder called

hysteria, an ancient malady that seems to have spawned different symptoms in different eras. In Freud's day, patients suffered from paralyzed limbs and fainting spells. Was what I was seeing and hearing at the conference—and in my own office—hysteria in another form?

It wasn't long into the question-and-answer period following the last speaker's presentation before a subject that was on my mind and, I would guess, the minds of most of the therapists in the audience, was finally broached. Had any of the therapists on the panel ever been harassed or even hurt by members of the groups from which their patients had escaped? Had they ever heard of such an incident? Was there a danger and, if so, how great was it?

The answer reassured me. Some of the therapists said they had either received dead animals in the mail or knew of others who had. In a few cases, there were reports of anonymous threats. But to their knowledge, no therapist had been harmed.

Finally, the session on ritual abuse ended. At first the audience was silent. Then, gradually, I could hear a rustling as my colleagues and I struggled to gather ourselves. The sense of shock in the room was palpable.

After a few more minutes, someone suggested that a poll be taken of how many in the audience were treating patients who said they had been ritually abused.

I looked around the room. There were perhaps 200 people in attendance, and all but a handful, I believed, were therapists. Almost everyone had a hand in the air.

Someone got up and thanked the participants for sharing their stories and their experiences. Then, slowly and quietly, we all filed out.

Chapter 12

RANDALL

RANDALL was tall, at least 5′9″, and one of the thinnest women I had ever seen. She must have weighed less than 100 pounds, which would have made her about 50 pounds underweight. Her short blond hair was parted on one side. She wore no makeup and no jewelry, not even earrings, and at our first session was dressed in chinos, sneakers, a white button-down shirt and a brown leather bomber jacket, all of which made her look more like a teenaged boy than the 28-year-old woman she was.

She shook my hand and I ushered her down the hall to my office. I pointed to the bentwood chair and suggested she take a seat, which she did. As I walked around her to my chair, I noticed that she still had her jacket on.

Randall had called for the appointment a few days earlier, saying that she had gotten my name from one of her co-workers at a child-abuse agency. As she settled in her chair, I made a point of not saying anything, in case she wanted to start the session. But getting no immediate response, I began in my usual manner.

"How can I be of assistance?"

"I do this thing with food," she said. "I really don't understand it, but I've been doing it for as long as I can remember."

I waited for her to continue.

"It's complicated. I don't know where to start."

"Start any place," I said. "Just say whatever comes into your mind about it, in any order."

"Well, first of all I believe that I'm too fat. I look at myself in the mirror and I see an overweight person. But, you know, all my friends tell me that I'm way too thin. I'll go on a diet anyway, and then, right in the middle of it, I'll binge. I'll just go to the refrigerator and instead of eating a piece of something, which is my intention, I'll just stay there and eat all of it. I can eat an entire pizza, a Sara Lee chocolate cake and a quart of ice cream at one sitting. I once went to the store for a bagel. I bought a dozen and ate all of them before I got home.

"After I do something like that, I feel terrible. Bloated. I can't stand it, so I throw up. It makes me feel better. But afterward, I hate myself. I hate myself so much I have to eat something to soothe myself. So you see, it just goes 'round and 'round.

"When I get into one of these moods, I sometimes start taking a lot of laxatives. Because I feel so bloated. Or I buy water pills in the drugstore. They make me feel better.

"And there's something else. I'm sort of embarrassed to talk about it."

Rather than reassure her, I was silent.

"Well, I might as well tell you all of it. I have this thing about odors—the way bodies smell. I'm constantly taking showers. Usually twice a day. Sometimes three or four times."

She lowered her voice.

"I douche constantly, and use a lot of deodorizers. My gynecologist told me to stop, because I was getting infections.

"And there's another thing. When I'm on a diet, I get so

hungry. But I don't want to gain any weight, so sometimes I eat inanimate things."

"Inanimate things?" I not so much asked as exclaimed in surprise.

"Like paper, pens. I can chew a pencil all the way down, except for the metal part around the eraser. That gives me trouble. Sometimes I will buy a yogurt, eat it, then eat the container, and the spoon."

"You eat the plastic spoon?" I said, not containing my astonishment.

"I seem to have very tough teeth. I can chew anything. It's sort of a mark of pride for me. I think of various things that I would like to try to eat. You know what I'd really like to try? I'd like to try to eat a car."

"How in God's name could you eat an automobile?"

"Listen, I've thought a lot about this. If I could break it down into small enough pieces, I could chew them all up. It would get me into the Guinness Book of Records."

Inanimate objects. That was a new one. I had treated anorexics, who starve themselves, and bulimics, who, like Randall, binge and then regurgitate. But I had never heard of anyone who fantasized so extensively about consuming inanimate objects, much less Buicks.

As we talked further, I learned that Randall had an inverse relationship with food. It consumed her. She thought about food constantly. To eat or not to eat? What to eat. Where to eat. Her favorite pastime was reading restaurant menus. The food section of *The New York Times* came next. Randall had preferences. She was a vegetarian and a health food advocate, with an aversion to meat and dairy products. Yet she said that sometimes she would stuff herself with hamburgers and Häagen-Dazs.

Randall grew up on a small farm in South Jersey. Her father was a cattle wholesaler. (Maybe that explained why she rarely ate meat, I thought to myself.) She had two older brothers but had not seen them in years. After graduating from a state college she became a third-grade teacher in

Jersey City. But she didn't like it and quit after a year. She went back to school, got a master's degree in social work and then a job at a methadone clinic. Later, she switched again to a job in which she found foster homes for abused children. She loved the work, she said, but it was heartrending and frustrating, since very often the foster home was worse than the child's original one, and then what do you do? Her tensions on the job, she believed, were at the root of her eating problem.

Randall said that she rarely drank and didn't smoke. Like Rebecca, she said that recreational drugs frightened her. She had a few close female friends and a few male friends in whom, she was careful to tell me, she had no romantic interest. She had never been married, rarely dated and claimed to have tried sex a few times while she was in college but didn't like it. For a while, she said, she had wondered whether she was a lesbian, but realized that she had never been attracted to another woman. Was she asexual or simply celibate? I decided to leave that for later, when our rapport was better.

Randall's parents had both died a short while earlier in an automobile wreck, an event I assumed had compelled her to seek me out now. Even though she was a social worker, and obviously knew she had a serious eating disorder, she had never been in therapy. I accepted her into treatment and we decided she would come twice a week, which she did regularly and punctually. She and I seemed to get along, and as we gradually got to know each other she told me a lot about her life. What was noticeably missing, however, was information about her formative years. She said she just did not remember much. This amnesia suggested that she might have been abused, something that did not really surprise me, since there is a high correlation between eating disorders and early childhood abuse.

One of the few memories Randall had of her childhood was of mealtimes, which she said were a horror. Her mother forced her to eat whatever was placed in front of her, even if she hated it. She would tell me about putting food in her mouth, pretending to chew it and then spitting it out in her hand when her mother wasn't looking. Or chewing and chewing without swallowing it, and then getting yelled at or hit by her mother, who seemed to insist on absolute control over her daughter. Indeed, Randall's mother decreed what clothes her daughter wore, even though her taste was out of phase with that of Randall and her friends. And her mother would not let Randall cut her hair, insisting on braiding it so tightly that it hurt. Randall told me that as soon as she would get out of the house she would unwind the braids, only to have someone redo them before she returned home.

Randall didn't talk much about her father, other than to insist that she loved him. It was her father, she said, who protected her from her mother. But it troubled her that, far from being devastated, she felt nothing at his death. In fact, she felt nothing at all. She experienced her parents' funeral, she said, as if it were a movie. At first, I thought that she surely had been overwhelmed by the shock. After all, both her parents died at the same time. But when I investigated it with her, she ashamedly told me that she was sort of happy that her mother was dead, and she did not mourn her. And for her father, she felt nothing. She knew there was something wrong with this, but that was how she felt.

OUR work progressed. Randall gained insight into her personality and her problems. As she saw how controlling her mother was, she realized how obsessed she had become with the one aspect of her life that she could control, her weight. And although she still thought she was too fat at 100 pounds, her compulsive eating and purging diminished.

I could not have asked for a more cooperative patient. She never missed a session. She was always on time, always willing to work. She had even gotten into the practice of leaving her leather jacket on the coat rack, symbolically taking off at least one of her protective layers.

And yet the missing years of her life were still missing. Whenever we tried to investigate them, she would develop unusual symptoms. Sometimes she would complain of spasms in her right arm or, even stranger, burning sensations. Saying that her arm felt as if it was on fire, she would go to the bathroom and splash cold water on it. When she came back, she would sometimes pick up the pillow from my couch and place it on her lap, like it was a shield. I did not have to be a Freud to get the metaphoric message—stay away.

And stay away I did. So we talked mostly about her job. She was deeply upset by the stories she heard from her young clients. And she was frustrated by the social service system that was supposed to investigate abuse but like many government bureaucracies was slow and ineffective. We talked about the difficulty of putting children on the witness stand to testify about abuse, and the horror of a child being cross-examined. Who was one to believe? The child? The parent? What if one parent was accusing the other of abusing the child just to gain a favorable divorce settlement? And all along I wondered if Randall wasn't also talking about herself.

After a few months of this, Randall told me she was having trouble sleeping. She would go to bed, fall asleep for a few hours but then be awakened by a nightmare. She never remembered the content of the dream, only that she was terrified, sometimes so much so that she would wake up screaming. It seemed to her that she had traded an eating disorder for nightmares, and she was starting to fear that therapy, by stirring up things and not resolving them, was to blame.

"I've been thinking," Randall told me at the start of one session, brushing her short blond hair back from her face.

"We know there are missing periods in my life. Times that I have no memories for. Every time we try and look at that period, I have some sort of terrible reaction. You see it in the office. And I feel awful for days afterward. Now I'm not sleeping. My work is suffering. I'm not exactly ignorant of this process. I am a social worker, and I have an idea what all this must mean. Look, Dr. Mayer, isn't there something you can do? What about hypnosis? Do you think you could hypnotize me? You have to do something, because I can't take much more."

Randall's resistance had been formidable, and I had respected it. By joining it, and not confronting it, the resistance had only gotten worse. But perhaps her unconscious had wanted it that way. Perhaps her unconscious was using her pain, her fears, her nightmares, to push Randall to look at what for all this time she had refused to face. The iron was almost hot, I thought to myself. I decided to leave it in the fire a little longer.

"I haven't slept more than four hours a night for the last three months," Randall said. And she looked like it, too. Her face was even more gaunt than usual. "I don't know how I can keep going."

"Perhaps we should send you to a psychiatrist who can prescribe medication to help you sleep," I suggested.

"Absolutely not. That would be admitting I can't deal with it, that I'm not strong enough to deal with my anxiety without a crutch. Look what I did with food. It would be the same thing. No, I can't use sleeping pills. That would feed into that part of me that I wanted therapy to eliminate. You should be helping me more. Maybe you're the one who's afraid. Maybe you're frightened of what we will find," she said fiercely.

My patient was now demanding that I force her to delve into her suppressed memories. The gods of therapy be thanked.

"Would you like to go into hypnosis right now, or should

we wait until next time?" I asked her. It was a standard technique to get additional conscious cooperation. Either way she answers, she is agreeing to enter hypnosis.

"Let's get it over with."

Randall went into a trance without much fuss, her lean frame slumping in the bentwood chair. Because her resistance had been so strong, I took the time to have her construct a safe room, to give her a place where she could feel as secure as possible. She wanted the walls to be covered with lead shields. And the room had television monitors so she could see anyone coming toward it. Once she was inside, I asked her to go to the part of the room where there were shelves of videotapes of the years she didn't remember. Then I instructed her to pick one of the cassettes and put it in the VCR. I told her to settle back in her chair and tell me what she saw.

"There is a little girl on the screen," Randall said quietly. "She looks like me. She's about eleven. She is playing in my bedroom. I can see out the window. That's the grassy field outside, where the cows go in the summer. I remember it. I always liked looking out that window.

"Her mother comes in and tells her that she should get ready to go out. Something just happened to the little girl. She looks different. She looks scared. I don't understand. It's not me anymore."

"Who is it now?"

"I don't know."

"Ask her."

"How can I ask someone on a TV screen?"

"Go ahead," I assured her. In a hypnotic state apparent inconsistencies can be resolved with a little encouragement. "Go on. She'll answer."

I waited a few moments. Then Randall began to speak, slowly and softly.

"She says her name is Alice and her job is to do whatever her mother tells her to do."

"What happens next?"

"They both get into a car. It looks like they are going south. Then the mother stops the car and takes out a black hood. She puts it over the girl's head and ties it shut."

"It's dark. I can't see."

Randall had shifted from the third person to the first. She was rocking back and forth nervously in the chair.

"I know that something terrible is going on. Someone, please help me."

"Where are you?"

"I don't know. It feels like I'm in a car and we're moving. Something is over my head. I can't see out. It's hard to breathe."

"What do they call you?"

"My name is Bat Girl. I have no eyes, but I can tell what is happening by sensing it, hearing it. I come out whenever we are in a dark place."

Well, it certainly was a cleverly descriptive name.

"Does that happen often?" I asked.

"When we drive mother puts a hood over her head. That's when I come out. She's scared of the dark. I'm not. Since I have no eyes, it doesn't matter to me."

She sat quietly for a few moments. Then I saw her body contort, and I realized she was getting out of the car.

"What's happening now?"

"I'm being led into a room where I will be undressed. Mother is talking."

"What is she saying?"

" 'This is a very important night. Tonight you are going to be initiated. You are to do exactly what you are told or it will be very bad for you. You know what will happen.' 'Yes mother, I know,' I tell her."

With a slender hand, Randall brushed her blond hair off her face.

"Then she took the hood off and went away. The room was dark. I sat there for a long time. I don't know how long. Then I heard someone whimpering. It came from some-place nearby, in the room. But I couldn't see anyone. I listened hard. It was dark, but it didn't bother me. I had been here before. There were more sounds, from a different place in the room. Another little girl? I crawled around until I found the first one and touched her. I told her that it was okay and that I would be right back. Then I went to the other side and found another little girl. I took her hand and led her back to the first one. The first girl's name was Annie. The second was named Sally.

"Annie said that she had been brought to the room the night before. It was after she was told to kill a little baby. She couldn't do it, so they then put her in the room and told her that she would be next. She was afraid. Sally said that this was the first time that she was here. She didn't know why. She was afraid, too.

"I knew then what was going to happen. One of them was going to be sacrificed, and I was going to have to do it. If I didn't, I would be the sacrifice. They would kill me, either that night or the next time."

Randall suddenly got out of her chair and started to pace back and forth, her chinos flapping around her thin legs. Apparently, she had switched into another personality, one who walked—and talked—rapidly.

"If I don't kill one of them, they will kill me. If I do kill one, I am the murderer. I would be one of them. I don't want to be one of them, but I am. I have killed before. No, I didn't kill, someone else did. Someone else held my hand on the knife. But I should have resisted. I should have tried. But it was impossible."

I had heard a tale like this before. I thought of Ned. And Rebecca. I wondered about the similarity of the episodes my patients were telling me.

"Who are you now?" I asked quietly.

"I am Confusion. Every time I think of a solution, I find an objection to it. So I am always confused."

Just as I was thinking that it sounded like Alice in Wonderland, I heard a much deeper voice from my patient, who by now had returned to the bentwood chair and was sitting, her legs crossed and her face composed.

"I will settle it."

"Who are you?"

"I am Julius, after Julius Caesar, who debated before he crossed the Rubicon."

How a child could know about Julius Caesar I had no idea. Maybe she named this alter later. Maybe she had studied him in school.

"He did it. I can do it. I always know what is best to do. I am always fighting with her. Confusion, I mean. Sometimes I can push her out of the way, sometimes she pushes me. We always battle for control. I will stop this debate. I will decide what to do tomorrow. Tonight, I will not think about it. I will just hold the girls until they go to sleep."

She sunk into her chair and was quiet for a little while. But then she jumped up, as if she had been startled by something.

"The door is opening." She had switched back to Confusion's staccato voice. "A big person comes in. His face is covered, so I can't see who he is. He takes my hand. Another man goes over to Annie and takes her out of the room. And Sally, too. Then I am taken out.

"We go to a big room. With a table in the center. They put both girls in front of the table and tell me to choose one of them. Which one? Annie or Sally? Which one?"

"Eenie, meanie, minie, moe." It was the Julius voice. I guess he was not as decisive as his namesake. "Catch a tiger by the toe. My mother says to pick this one. Y . . . O . . . U.

"It was Annie. They put her on the table and tied her down." It was a another voice. I was not sure who was speaking. "There are other people there. They are all wearing masks. They make me stand in front of the table. I am naked. One of them says to me, 'You have chosen. Now you are one of us. There is no going back.' They are all singing. I can't understand the words. They do it for a long time.

Then one of the people pours something from a pitcher on Annie. It's blood. She shrieks. He hits her hard, on the mouth.

"Then he goes over to the other side of the room and picks up a knife. He brings it back and hands it to me."

Randall shuddered, signaling another switch. I asked her who was speaking.

"I am Shield," she said, in an emotionless voice. "I protect her from all of this. My job, which I hate, is to shield her and let the others come out who can do this work."

"The others?"

"There is Obsidian, who is cold and black, like the stone. She is not evil, but she reflects what is around her. And Misty. She leaves the body and floats around the room. Nothing can harm her, since she has no substance. There is the one that does the killing. She has done it before. She has no feelings. She is like a machine and simply does it. There are the Many Selves and the Many Pockets, whose job it is to absorb the horrible things and who take the sex."

Quite a group, I thought to myself. Maybe the complexity was a response to the degree of abuse.

"I go inside to guard Randall. She is terrified. She doesn't know what to do. She is looking at Annie. Annie is looking at her. Confusion comes back out and thinks about killing herself, or killing the leader, or dropping the knife and running. The people are waiting, silently.

"I will do it," said a new voice, an eerie voice with a power I had felt a few times before with other patients. It didn't frighten me, as Helen's Evil One did. It was more like Rebecca's priestess personality, Artonoxima. I felt awe. So much so, in fact, that it was unnerving.

"I am Kalita. I am named after the great Goddess Kali. I have participated in many ceremonies. I know what to do."

She picked up an imaginary knife and stabbed the air in front of her.

"I did it well. I hope they are pleased. And now for the essence. I must take it."

She made some thrusting motions that I realized were a grotesque pantomime in which she broke into a chest from under the rib cage and pulled out an imaginary heart. She held the object in her two hands and walked a few steps to the right.

"Here it is, sir. I have done it."

She stood before me, erect and still. Then she reached her hand out to receive something, put it in her mouth, chewed and swallowed. She did it quickly and without apparent emotion. After a few moments, she raised her right hand up and, with her palm facing out, spread her little finger apart from the other four.

"One by one, the people come up and bow to me," she said, resuming her grisly narration. "Then they take me into the next room for the union."

"The union?" I heard myself ask. But I knew what was coming. There were differences to the rituals I have heard my patients describe, but most of them ended with sexual abuse. Satanism seemed to be a way to legitimize this perversion.

"The union. Men are to have intercourse with me, to unite me to the covenant. It is a great honor, but I don't partake in that. That is the job of Many Pockets."

With that, she seemed to shrink in size. Another voice spoke next.

"We are the Many Selves and the Many Pockets. It is our job to have sex with many people. We can become many selves, so that we don't feel anything. We have many pockets in our body, so that we can take a lot and don't feel anything. We are shaped like an accordion, with lots of folds, so we just keep separating into different pockets. As soon as we get home, we will unfold, and empty all of the pockets."

"How will you do that?" I asked.

"We will throw up the pieces of heart. We will wash out our body with laxatives, douches and enemas. They tell us that this places Satan inside us. But we fooled them. We never let it stay inside. We get rid of it."

"How did you know how to do those things?" I asked. After all, she was supposed to be a child.

"They taught us. We were given them since we were very little. They would do it to us before the desecration ceremony."

"What is that?"

"Where they would give us these things and then have us make on a cross or some other holy object. Sometimes we would try to fool them and hold out. It gave us a sense of pride to hold out for a little longer, to make them wait."

Small victory, I thought, but a victory that may have helped preserve them. Anyway, the cause of Randall's eating disorder—of the vomiting, laxatives, enemas, douches, water pills—seemed evident. It was a response to the sexual abuse and, if she could be believed, to the cannibalism. The gorging could also be an identification with the hedonistic nature of Satanism. Other patients told me they gluttonously engaged in food or sex.

Randall was wiping her hands over her body, as if to wash something off.

"The last one who was on top of us picks us up and takes us back into the room. 'You did well,' he says. 'Put your clothes on.' "

"Who was talking to you?"

"The leader."

"Do you recognize him?"

"I can't look at his face."

"Turn around and look at him."

She slowly turned her head and with that let out a scream.

"It's Daddy, it's Daddy."

At this point, she changed back to Randall. I helped her back to her chair and let her sit there for a few moments while I thought about what to do next. It had all happened so fast, I did not have time to make a plan.

"Stay in the trance while I talk to you, Randall. You've uncovered a lot of frightening information. You have kept it hidden all these years. When you come out of the trance you might remember some of it. You might remember all of it. You might not remember any of it. You might remember what happened but leave the feelings behind. You might slowly remember it, over the next few weeks, as you are able. Let your system decide what is best for you.

"Now, slowly, at your own pace, come back into this room." Anxiously, I waited.

Chapter 13

"IT'S MY JOB"

I had been fired. To make it worse, the news came in the mail.

The letter from Randall, which arrived several weeks after our eventful session, told me she was quitting therapy, effective immediately. She thanked me for all I had done and assured me that she was much better for having seen me. Yes, she wrote, she knew there were issues she still needed to work on. But for now, she was choosing to stop. Saying good-bye was always hard for her, she wrote. That's why she was doing it in a note.

I phoned her the day I got her letter. Whether or not she continued therapy was obviously not my decision, I told her, but I thought she should come in for at least one last session, to get some closure on the work we had done.

She thanked me for my concern. Then, politely but firmly, she said no.

I had hoped that by bringing her back I might find out which of her personalities wanted to quit. The only thing I could think to do now was to write Randall telling her that she could come in for that final session whenever she wanted. At least it would hold the door open. I did not get a response.

It hardly surprised me. The evening after she abreacted the satanic ritual had been particularly rough. Randall had nightmares all night and phoned me several times. I tried to calm her by telling her they were only dreams, and that they were triggered by events that happened long ago. But I was unable to help her separate the past from the present. I suggested that she come in the next day to talk about it. Until then, I said, she should turn on the television and all the lights in her apartment. That helped a little, but every time she tried to sleep she woke up with another nightmare, which was followed by another call to me. I suggested a warm bath. And a glass of hot milk. But Randall didn't really calm down until a friend mercifully arrived to spend the rest of the night with her.

In our emergency session the next day, and in many sessions that followed it, we talked about her memory. At first Randall doubted such horrible things could have happened to her, and perhaps because of the gruesome episodes I was already hearing from Rebecca and Helen, I wanted to believe that her memories were metaphoric rather than actual. But over the weeks I met several more internal personalities who filled in some of the blanks in her childhood. Like pieces in a puzzle, it fit together. They told of rapes by her father. There were hazy recollections of strange and violent ceremonies in candle-lit rooms. One of these personalities recalled an episode in which a newborn baby was baptized with blood instead of holy water. These revelations rattled Randall, but she pushed on. She said she wanted to know.

Interestingly, during this time her eating problems subsided further. They rarely came up for discussion in our sessions, and her weight appeared to be constant. I asked her about it once. She said that even though she still considered herself fat, she didn't think about it as often as before and no longer felt compelled to do anything about it.

All was going so well with the case that some pessimistic part of me wasn't at all surprised by Randall's letter firing me. Her view, I guess, was that since her symptoms had been alleviated and she had some understanding of her problem she was satisfied. I felt differently, but she was the boss. I worked for her and could be fired by her at any time. And I had to admit, Randall was functioning much better now. Her nightmares had stopped. And she found another job in a social work agency that helped the aged. Running group therapy sessions for senior citizens was much less problematic and frustrating for her than finding foster homes for abused children. In what I didn't know then were the closing days of our therapy, Randall talked about how much she liked her new position and how much good she thought she was doing. Who was I to judge her for stopping?

But judge her I did. It was mainly the abruptness with which she halted therapy that suggested something was wrong. In my postmortem on the case, I blamed myself. I had let myself be swayed by Randall's desire to go faster. Her abreaction happened too soon, before I could help her prepare for it. I had not sufficiently respected her resistance. I would know better the next time.

As my practice got busier, Randall's case gradually receded from my thoughts. My book on multiple personality disorder, *Through Divided Minds*, had been published, and I was getting phone calls from all over the country. People identified with the patients I wrote about, suspected that they were multiples and sought my advice. I would listen to their stories and refer them to someone I knew or had heard of in their area. I was also in demand as a speaker, presenting what the profession calls grand rounds, which are weekly lectures at hospitals and psychotherapeutic treatment centers. It was gratifying to be called in as an expert on a subject that only a few years before people—at some of those same places—insisted hardly existed. After my talks, I would often get calls from psychiatrists, psychologists and social workers requesting assistance with a case.

Then, one evening, as I was working on a lecture I was going to give at Coney Island General Hospital on "Recognizing and Diagnosing Multiple Personality Disorder," I heard my machine answer the phone. "Dr. Mayer, this is Randall," the voice on the line said. "I'd like to make an appointment to see you, if it's all right."

I was stunned. It had been over a year since she had quit. I picked up the phone in time to catch her and we arranged an appointment.

Two days later Randall was back in my bentwood chair, her wiry frame even more taut from exercise. She filled me in on what had happened during the past year. For the first few months she felt fine. That was hardly surprising— when a person stops therapy the pot ceases to boil. But then Randall began to have memories of other abusive and disturbing episodes. Predictably, her symptoms started to return. She went back to bingeing and throwing up, and soon the crazy diets, laxatives and water pills had resumed. Recognizing that this was not healthy, she tried to dissociate and calm herself in a better way. She became an exercise-aholic, joining a health club and working out for several hours every day. She was very strict about it. She even bought a stationary bicycle for her apartment. When she woke up with a nightmare—yes, she was having them again, too—she would jump on the bike, put on her Walkman and pedal until she was tired enough to sleep.

"Why didn't you call me when you started to have trouble?" I asked her.

"I was too embarrassed. I know that I didn't stop therapy the right way. I ran away from you. I know. And I was afraid you would be angry at me and refuse to see me again. Anyway, for a while I thought working out was the answer.

It made me feel better. I think it's the endorphins. You know, the runners' high. And maybe it would have been enough. But then I got this new symptom."

She paused, waiting for me to encourage her to continue, which I did with a nod.

"I really didn't want to talk about this, but . . . well . . . sometimes I have this desire to cut myself. Sometimes I want to cut my right arm."

I had heard other therapists talk about self-mutilators but had not treated one, although I once had a patient who would pull out clumps of her hair. The professional literature is full of reports of patients who do all sorts of nasty things to themselves—burning themselves with cigarettes, cutting designs in their flesh, inserting sharp objects into various orifices, even pouring oven cleaner on themselves. Sometimes the damage is superficial, but sometimes they hurt themselves badly enough to require hospitalization.

"It's hard to explain," Randall went on, "but I get these feelings. I don't know how to describe it, but I just know that if I cut myself I'll feel better. I know it sounds strange, but when I take out a razor blade and cut myself I feel better."

I realized that because she cut herself on her arm her new activity was not noticeable, since the wounds were covered by her shirt. "But doesn't it hurt?" I asked, quite unanalytically.

"Actually, it feels good. I can't explain, really, but some sort of pressure builds up inside me. I feel awful. I want to eat, but know it's wrong. Sometimes exercise helps, sometimes not. Then I hear something inside me saying, 'Get a razor and cut yourself. You'll feel better. You always do.' So I get a blade and, it's so strange, sometimes I just watch myself. The blade goes over the arm. The blood comes out in a thin line. I sit there and watch it. It feels good. Sometimes, I don't even remember doing it."

"Somebody else must be doing it," I said, thinking aloud.

"I guess so."

"Can I talk to that person?"

Randall nodded her agreement, then brushed a short strand of blond hair off her face. I put her in a light trance—she had always been highly hypnotizable—and sought out the alter. This was the good thing about working with a patient like Randall. It can take months to find out why a nonmultiple patient cuts himself. With a multiple, you simply ask to speak to the alter responsible.

"You wanted me?" a deep voice said.

"I understand that you are to blame for this cutting. Is that true?"

"Yes. Sometimes I can get her to do it. But when she won't, I push her out of the way and do it myself."

"How come she doesn't feel any pain?"

"There is pain, naturally, but the cutting is good for her, so she doesn't feel it. In fact, it makes her feel good."

"I don't understand."

"Well, when you do something that you shouldn't do, you're supposed to get punished. If you know you shouldn't have done it and feel guilty, then punishment helps. It alleviates the problem. She deserves it, and she knows she deserves it. So the punishment cancels out her crimes and everything is all right again. She feels good. Get it?"

It was sort of logical, in a convoluted way. Randall was punishing herself for sins she believed she had committed. I immediately thought of her abreaction. As she remembered it, she had taken part in a murder. I did not fully believe her story, but she clearly did. And it was more than reason enough to feel guilt.

I didn't relish having to deal with a patient who was carving herself up while I was trying to cure her. It might turn into a race. I decided to see if I could stop it, at least temporarily.

"Don't you think it's wrong to hurt someone?"

"Not if they deserve it."

"But she's already been through so much. Don't you think it's wrong to give her more pain?"

"I told you. She deserves it. I would like her to feel even more. To really be hurt. But she thinks it's good. Sometimes I cut her when she doesn't know it, so she will see it later and know that I am still here. My job is to remind her of what she has done."

"I think I know how you feel, and you obviously see that I disagree. But look, our time is almost up for today. Would it be possible for us to have an agreement that you won't cut her anymore until we have a chance to talk about this again?"

Surprisingly, the voice consented. I would like to think that it was my persuasive personality, but it was probably an indication that the Slasher was in need of help.

"The first thing we have to do is to deal with this cutting business," I said to Randall after I brought her out of the trance. "I think it stems from the events we were working on when you stopped therapy. The incidents you were trying to forget. I think that we have to go in and take a look at them. Sometimes the only way around these things is through them. But I have to warn you, Randall, it won't be pleasant and it won't be easy. If there was any other way to help you without making you delve into all this, I would do it. But I think you know by now there isn't."

"You're telling me that I have to go back? To Annie?"

It was the first time she had mentioned the child's name.

"Yes, to go back to Annie. We got the bare outlines of the memory last year, Randall, but many feelings were left behind. They were stirred up and wanted to come out— needed to come out—but you were frightened. You did what you could to avoid them. That's why I think you quit."

I paused to let my words sink in. I realized now that Randall's abreaction had only been partial. In order for an abreaction to be successful, the episode has to be relived completely, with all of the feelings that should have been experienced at the time. If these feelings are left behind again, they will continue to fester, like a partially drained boil that becomes reinfected.

"I could send you for a consultation with someone else, Randall, if you'd like. Why don't you think about it?"

"I don't want a consultation with anyone else," she said. She looked determined, almost grim. "I know you're right. I might as well do it now. Yes, let's do it now. This is the best time."

Given her reaction to the abreaction the first time, I wondered whether she was as ready as she insisted. She was sitting there, absently playing with her hair. Although I was sure that taking her back through the ritual was necessary, it was hardly without risk. The most common mistake the therapists I supervised make is allowing their patients to have abreactions too quickly. I had made that mistake myself with Ned and again with Randall. Was I about to do it once more? This time, I decided, I would err on the other side. We would approach our goal more slowly. Randall sounded as if she wanted to do it yesterday, and it was natural for her to want to get it behind her as quickly as possible. But she would have to be patient if this time it was going to work.

"You've been out of therapy for more than a year, Randall," I said, applying the brakes. "I need time to get to know you again."

For the next several weeks we rebuilt the relationship between us. I still wasn't sure to what extent, if any, she had been ritually abused. But it seemed likely that her father had repeatedly raped her, and the mother had allowed it. In addition, the mother was tyrannical, controlling Randall's day-to-day life and acting in a way that demonstrated that she hated her daughter, perhaps because her husband seemed to prefer his daughter to his wife. Anyway, Randall had a clearer view of her parents now. Most of her illusions were gone. She was angry at them. The resolution of anger is either vengeance, which, we know from Melville, does not always work, or forgiveness, which demands a spirituality most people do not have, or at least an understanding of an abuser's motivation. Having parents who are alive helps, since there is the possibility of communication and understanding. But in Randall's case, of course, there was no such possibility, since her parents were dead. So the best that could be hoped for was that she would come to take a Mafia-like position on the matter: Forgive, but don't forget.

Unfortunately, the contract I made with the slasher personality did not hold. He called me one evening and said that enough was enough. He was going to cut her arm again. I tried to find out why, but he wouldn't tell me. In retrospect, I think we were probably getting too close to Randall's past, frightening her and causing her to push me away, or at least create a diversion. I reminded the personality that he had promised not to cut her until he talked to me. He said that was what he was doing now and hung up. I wished I had added the phrase, "in person" to our contract. Or remembered how literal the unconscious mind is.

Randall told me at her next session that he had cut her on her right inner thigh. I asked to talk to the Slasher, but he wouldn't come out. I guess he suspected that I was going to trick him. At any moment, I realized, Randall could severely injure herself. I had run out of options, and time. We had to push ahead. We had to go through the abreaction again.

I set aside the following Friday evening for the session. That way, we could go on for as long as we needed, and Randall would have the weekend to recuperate.

"I want you to go back to about a year ago," I suggested, after putting Randall into a light trance. "Do you remember the safe room that you built? The one in which you sat and watched the videotape on the television. You saw something on that tape that happened to you a long time ago, when you were a girl. You were sleeping in your room and your mother came in to take you out. Do you remember?''

"I was Alice. And mother was coming in to take us to that place again.''

Randall started to squirm in her chair, and I suspected she had switched to Alice, who I remembered from the first abreaction. Instead of toying with her hair, as Randall did, she fiddled with her fingernails, picking at the cuticles.

"Where is Randall?" I asked.

"Inside. She's too frightened. That's why I came out. I can do whatever mother asks and not show how scared I am. She does bad things when we are scared.''

I noted that she had gone from watching the imaginary tape to re-enacting the scene, without any prompting from me. It gave me a little more confidence. I pushed on.

"What sort of things?''

"She hits us. If we cry, she hits us harder. Sometimes she uses a belt.''

Alice continued through the episode, coming to the part where the hood was put over her head and she became Bat Girl. I asked her if Randall was listening to what was going on. Instead of answering, she appeared to switch.

"Randall is that you?''

"Yes, only I am much younger. I am eleven. They call me Randy. I don't want to be here. Why am I here? I am never here.''

I guessed Randy was probably a fragment, since I hadn't encountered her before.

"I want you to watch it all this time, Randy. If it gets too much for you, you can go away. But try to watch as much of it as you can. Can you do that?''

When we got to the part where she found the other two girls, I met another personality who did not take part in the first abreaction. She called herself Sandra and she was the one who had spent the night with the two other children. She remembered having conversations with them. Annie knew that she was going to be killed, because she had failed to perform her part in the ritual the night before. Sandra said she promised to kill her quickly, so Annie would not feel much pain. In return, Annie promised to try not to scream. She said that she forgave Sandra because she knew that there was no choice. She understood that she would be killed anyway, and Sandra might as well try to save herself.

The grim story proceeded until we got to the part where Julius made the choice and Shield came out to protect Randall. She was slumped in her chair, looking ashen. I intervened at this point.

"Shield?"

"Yes?"

"I want you to step aside and not protect Randy this time."

"I always wanted to step aside. I did not want to stay around. But the others would not let me."

Then the body, who I assumed at this point to be Randy, let out a shriek that I thought would alarm the neighbors. Just as quickly she became quiet. She sat straight up in the chair, her tall, thin body assuming a calm, almost regal presence I recognized from before. It was Kalita.

"It is my job," she said. "I will sacrifice the child."

As she had done a year earlier, the patient went through her murderous pantomime, picking up an imaginary knife and holding it as if she was about to plunge it into someone. This time, I stopped her.

"Kalita, do you remember me?"

"Yes. You're her doctor. Don't you want me to show you again how I did it?"

"Yes, but I want to talk to you first. Why did you come out?"

"Why not? It's my job. The killing. She is incapable of it," she said evenly. "Besides, I like performing in the rituals. And this is an important one. If it goes well, I will be rewarded."

"I noticed last time that you did it quickly. Why?"

"I wanted to show them how well I could do my job. I wanted to show them that I don't flinch. I don't show emotion. That I am a professional."

"Did you look in Annie's eyes?" I asked.

"Yes. She was afraid. She had her chance. She should have done her job better." She spoke like a teacher explaining a student's failing grade.

"Look in her eyes again now. Do you feel anything?"

"I feel nothing," she said, surveying me with cool eyes. "Anyway, what's the purpose of all these questions? You're holding us up."

"I'm sorry, but I have to ask them," I said, as dispassionately as possible. "Now tell me, what happens after you stab her?"

"Like always. The blood spurts up. You have to turn away so you don't get it on you. Then the heart is removed."

"How do you get the heart out?" I asked, fighting my nausea.

"With a child it's easy, since the ribs are still soft. With older people it can be difficult. Then the men have to help."

"Why the heart?"

"Don't you know anything? It's important to eat the heart of the person who is sacrificed. To be sacrificed is a high honor. To ingest the most important organ of the sacrifice is to obtain power from that person."

"I wonder if you could step aside and let Randy do it?" I asked, not sure I really wanted her to comply.

"Why? It's my job. And she can't do it. She's too soft."

"Is that why you did it? To protect her?"

She didn't answer me directly. She simply said that if I wanted her to, she would step aside. I wondered why she was so cooperative. Probably she didn't like to eat hearts and was just acting tough.

"Randy, I want you to pick up the knife. Look into Annie's eyes. Do what you have to do."

Randall was sitting on the couch. I was in a chair right next to her. For such a tall woman she had an amazing ability to make herself seem small. She was all scrunched up, her feet pulled under her with her hands clutching her toes. Her eyes were wide with fear.

"I'll hold your hand, if you like." I said.

She reached out, grabbed my right hand and squeezed hard.

"Annie, Annie. Poor Annie. Forgive me, Annie. I have no choice. I will do it fast so you don't suffer. I will remember you, always. Please forgive me, Annie."

With that she made a stabbing motion and started to scream again. In between screams, she made these guttural noises that were impossible to understand. My hand hurt. So did my ears, despite the plugs I had put in, a precaution I learned to take from past abreactions.

As she re-enacted eating the heart, a disgusted look came over her face. It was hard for her to chew and even harder to swallow. For a moment I thought she might vomit in my office.

I thought of that first abreaction with Rebecca, the one in which she stabbed the pillow on my analytic couch with an imaginary knife and then acted out a gruesome pantomine in which she appeared to carve out a heart, cut it into pieces and pass it to the "devils" she said were gathered around her. Now, as then, I felt queasy. But I knew that I had to help my patient re-live the full experience, however shaken we both felt. I had to control my nausea and hers. I had to help her get all of the feelings out now, so we wouldn't have to go through this again.

I went to turn up the volume.

"That's right, chew it all. Remember what the consistency felt like. Remember what it tasted like. Remember what it smelled like. Chew it. Swallow it. I know it's hard. I know it's horrible. You want to throw it up. Don't, because they will kill you. That's right, swallow it."

She made more swallowing gestures.

"That's good," I said. "It's almost over. You'll never have to do it again."

Suddenly, she switched back to Kalita. It must have been too intense. It gave me an opportunity to be even more thorough.

"You are being cruel. Why did you make her do that? Wasn't it bad enough that she had to do it the first time? That's why I came out."

"So you came out to protect her?"

With this, Kalita lost some of her composure. "Well . . . I guess so. I always thought . . . I'm confused. What have you done to me?"

"It's all right," I said. "You came out because you knew that she couldn't do it. She switched into you so that this horrible thing could be done. You saved her life; you protected her."

"I thought I did it because I wanted to be a success. I wanted them to like me. I wanted to be part of it."

"I don't think so. It may seem that way to you, but I think you really did it to protect her, to save all of you. They owe you a great deal."

"You have confused me. I need to think this through. May I go now?"

"Yes, but let's talk again about this. Remember, you did your job and you did it well."

The rest of the abreaction was loud and terrible but essentially anticlimactic. Randall experienced the horror and pain of the rapes, the feeling of being utterly helpless. As we went through it, she lay on her back on my couch, screaming up at the ceiling while I sat beside her, holding her hand, encouraging her to experience her helplessness. Sweat poured from her. My hand ached. Even with earplugs my ears hurt from her screams. Finally, still holding onto my hand, she was convulsed by tears. After two and a half hours, it was over. I was exhausted. I couldn't imagine what she felt like.

She couldn't go home right away, of course, so I let her sit on the couch, gathering herself.

"Let's leave this place and come back into the office," I

said after a few moments. I helped her up from the couch and led her to the bentwood chair, which she sort of collapsed into. I hoped moving her from one place to another would somehow help separate the past from the present.

After a while Randall looked at me. "That's why I can't eat meat," she said without much feeling. "I hate those bastards."

I understood, but said nothing.

Chapter 14

COLLEEN

COLLEEN had the strangest job of any of my patients. She was an "M" in an "S and M" parlor, a person paid for being abused. She said it was better than doing it for love, and she spoke from experience.

She was a dark-haired, blue-eyed, strikingly handsome woman who wanted to be an actress. And from time to time Colleen would win a part in an Off- or Off-Off-Broadway play. But they were strictly minor-league productions, offering the possibility a critic might see her but nothing else other than a small percentage of the profits, if there were any. There never were.

The paradox of her profession was that she spent more money on it than she earned from it. There were acting classes, dancing classes and voice classes. There was the photographer who took pictures for her constantly changing portfolio. There was the cost of copying each new version of her book and mailing it out, over and over again. There was even a wardrobe consultant who helped select her clothes and also coached her for interviews and open calls.

Colleen's teachers were convinced that she had talent and told her she would make it. All she needed was perseverance—and a few more years of lessons.

When she arrived in New York, Colleen waited on tables in expensive restaurants while pursuing her dream. It was a perfect job for an aspiring actress. It paid reasonably good money, most of it in cash. She could choose her hours to coincide with classes and rehearsals and, if she got a part, she could take off a few days. The shows never ran longer than that anyway. And even if they did, she could always get another job in another restaurant. The city is filled with them.

But then Colleen fell in love. His name was Don and he was a floor trader for a major stock brokerage. He was tall and dark and came from a well-bred New England family. She met him one evening when he came into her restaurant and sat at one of her tables.

Colleen later told me she would try anything once. That was fine with Don. She let him spank her and tie her up and play out various scenes that they read about in sado-masochistic books such as the *Story of O*. To her surprise, Colleen enjoyed it.

Gradually they had escalated their play, becoming involved in sado-masochism clubs that had opened around New York City in the 1970s. They met other couples with similar proclivities and exchanged notes. The stories she told me about this time were, to say the least, bizarre. And I must confess I found it degrading for her. Don seemed to have a deep hatred for women that he took out on Colleen. Sometimes he would require her to be silent, beating her if she talked. Or he would put a collar around her neck and chain her naked in a room and order her to clean it. Once, at his country home in eastern Long Island, he chained her to a sled and made her pull him over the snow. Sometimes, he simply made Colleen beg for a beating.

For her part, Colleen had signed a "contract" committing herself into slavery to Don. There was even a clause that allowed him to hire her out to his friends, who could do what they wished with her.

"It was more exciting than any of my other relationships," she told me at one session. "S and M brings out the ultimate closeness between two people, allowing him to control me and trusting that he will stop if I ask him to."

No one had the right to judge them, Colleen insisted. They'd been consenting adults. And the physical abuse was not so strong as to require medical treatment.

There was another advantage for Colleen, too. With Don supporting her, she'd no longer had to wait tables and had plenty of time to pursue her acting, of which he was very supportive. In fact, their only disagreement was when Don wanted her to act in porno movies. Colleen hadn't been against it morally, but she felt it would hurt her chances for a legitimate role on Broadway, so she refused.

Colleen began to have second thoughts about Don, though, when he told her he wanted to bring another "slave" into the house. He was willing to make her subordinate to Colleen, but it was obvious to her that Don really wanted a harem. This was too much for Colleen, and she soon found herself alone, living in a tenement apartment on the Lower East Side.

But she had found something she liked to do that was far more lucrative than waiting tables. So she contacted some of the people she met with Don and found a job at an S and M parlor in lower Manhattan, which is where she was working when she first came to me for therapy.

M's were hard to find. It was much more common for women to be S's, dressing in black leather and abusing men for a fee. So Colleen was much in demand. She was paid $300 to $500 a session, depending on what she was willing to submit to. The sessions lasted about an hour, which meant that for only a day or two of work a week she could easily take home $2,000, tax free.

She could set limits on the abuse, and the sessions were always monitored by bouncers over closed-circuit television. Her clients, she told me, were generally corporate types. She felt she was doing something that was socially beneficial. These men needed something that they could not get at home. And, of course, Colleen enjoyed her work.

But Colleen was not at peace. Starting at about the time of her breakup with Don, she began having fragmentary but violent memories in which she was either about to be raped or physically abusing other people. Then came one particularly startling and horrifying flashback. She was in the midst of a roast chicken dinner. As she was chewing on a wing, she had the overpowering feeling that she was gnawing on a human finger.

She bolted from the table and walked around her neighborhood until she was exhausted. Then she went back to her apartment and put herself to bed, only to be awakened by a series of nightmares that continued for several more nights. She had one repetitive dream in which she would put her nightgown on the bed and hide in the corner of the room. Then, she would see her father come in, pick up the nightgown and commence to have sex with it. She would wake up from other dreams gasping for breath or with the feeling that something was in her mouth, choking her.

More memories were triggered by her acting lessons, which were designed to put her in touch with emotional experiences so that she could convey the emotions to her audience. Once, she was playing out a scene in which she was supposed to feel terror and using exercises her coach gave her to get in touch with the fear inside of her when she lost control and ran into the street screaming. A classmate caught up with her and calmed her down over coffee. Colleen told her about her dreams, including the one about her father. The friend, herself a childhood abuse victim, told Colleen about an incest survivors' group.

Colleen started attending meetings, hoping to find solace. But at first they triggered more disturbing memories. Then she heard a woman at one of the sessions talk about how there were other personalities inside her, and Colleen had a revelation: she, too, had other personalities living inside of her. Colleen realized that she had been switching into one of those alter personalities during her masochistic sessions and switching back after they were over, without knowing it. The alter was the masochist, not Colleen.

(Unconscious switching is not uncommon. As a result, multiples can feel as though they are here one moment and someplace else the next. And their sense of time is not linear. I once saw a woman who, in the midst of a consultation, switched into a frightened 14-year-old girl who wanted me to hold her hand. We talked for about 10 minutes and then she switched back to the original personality, who picked up our earlier conversation at the point she had left off, never realizing that she had switched. When I pointed it out to her, she didn't know what I was talking about.)

At one of the incest-group meetings, Colleen had heard someone discussing therapy with me. She'd made an appointment and had come to my office a few days later. She was dressed in silk, as if she walked out of a window at Saks Fifth Avenue. She was composed, too, but then she was an actress.

At that first session, she told me that she believed that she had been brought up in a cult in which the grandparents, parents and children all took part. But we spent most of those first weeks of therapy discussing her remarkable inner world, of which she was only then beginning to become fully aware. Colleen now believed she had more than a thousand internal personalities—she tried to keep track of them on a large chart on a wall of her apartment—who lived in what seemed like a fortified fairyland, complete with ornate castles. It was as though a door had opened to a room she had never been in. As Colleen looked around, she found more and more nooks and crannies, which she carefully categorized. She would take days off from work and spend them examining the internal terrain.

At one session, a personality who called herself the

Guide came out and gave me a tour. Each castle, the Guide said, housed groups of alters who had been subjected to similar kinds of abuse. There were other alters who were abusers, and they lived in yet another castle.

The castles sounded very much like they could be on the Rhine, except they were all in one internal town. They were connected by twisting streets that made the castles easy to defend. And on each street there was something of beauty—a little garden here, a lovely church there and so on.

Each castle was surrounded by a wide moat that also flowed into each of the structure's rooms. And each moat was connected to the moats of the other castles. The moats were all fed by six wells that sprung from a vast underground chamber. Each well represented an emotion: there was an anxiety well, an anger well, a sadness well, a terror well, a worry well and a helplessness well. Apparently the wells were reservoirs for feelings too powerful for the alters to contain. There was a separate group of alters who controlled the flow in this hydraulic emotional system.

Each castle had a wing where a number of governor and nurse personalities lived. Their job was to protect the others from memories that might be overpowering. Over the months as we worked in therapy, these personalities said they were releasing more and more memories and more and more feelings from the underground cistern. I was told not to worry, they knew how much the other personalities could handle. I came to think of them as emotional spigots.

Colleen's inner world also contained stables, aviaries and cages for animals that she said contained memories of acts too terrible for any human to have committed. She warned me that a lot of work was going to have to be done with these animals. I hadn't the slightest idea how, though, since of course they couldn't talk.

In the center of this bizarre but beautiful assemblage was the central palace, where the Guardian Angel, obviously

Colleen's inner self-helper, resided, along with what Colleen called the Council of the Bureaucrats. She said there were too many alters for a democracy, so the Angel served as an enlightened dictator, delegating authority to one chief personality in each castle. Among the bureaucrats, there was a scribe who recorded everything that happened and a corps of engineers to build new castles when they were needed.

The entire world was ringed by two walls, with yet another moat in between. On the walls were perched guardhouses in which enforcer personalities were stationed. Their job was to keep everything within the world secret and prevent outsiders from gaining admittance. The guide warned that we would have to work very carefully in order not to alarm the enforcers. They might kill in order to maintain the secrecy.

DESPITE the bewildering complexity and apparent booby traps of her inner world, Colleen was an easy patient to work with. Maybe too easy. She came to our sessions prepared to work. Intelligent and forthright, she presented no overt resistance. Indeed, by the time she came to me she had started to research multiple personality disorder. Her goal in therapy, she told me, was to access all her forgotten memories, then abreact them, then integrate the personalities. One, two, three. It made me feel like a hired hand. But after my experience with Randall, when she bolted from therapy for a year, I was prepared to slow Colleen down, if necessary.

Colleen told me she had been an army brat. Her father, a West Point graduate and career officer, moved around so much she could not claim any one place as home. She was born in North Carolina, but spent time in Texas, New Mexico, California and in Europe and the Middle East. She said she never spent more than two years in any one town. The best thing about moving around so much, she said, was the ability to make friends. That must have been true, for she was quite personable.

After high school and two years at a community college on the West Coast, Colleen said, she worked as a flight attendant. But after a few years she grew bored with the travel, which she felt was a repeat of her childhood. She said she wanted to put down roots. She was in New York when she decided this, and so she stayed. She wanted to be a model, but was told that at 24 she was too old. Acting was her next choice—Broadway was her top goal, followed by Hollywood and the soaps. Commercials were a distant fourth.

Colleen said she had only spotty memories of her early childhood. There were many missing chunks of time, and she was totally blank from age five to seven, when her father was stationed in San Francisco, and age nine, when he was stationed in West Texas, near the Mexican border. Here and there, however, she could recall a school that she went to or a friend.

Her father was now dead. Her mother lived in Charlotte, North Carolina, with her mother's older sister. Colleen had as little contact with her mother as possible. She would not visit her or return her telephone calls, even though she knew her mother was dying of cancer.

When I asked why, Colleen told me she was angry at her because of the abuse that she was remembering. When she confronted her mother about it, her mother said she didn't know what Colleen was talking about. She insisted that Colleen had a perfect childhood and did not understand why she seemed so troubled.

Colleen had a brother who was four years older and also was a soldier. When she asked him about her recollections of abuse, he just shook his head and told her not to talk about it. His reaction essentially confirmed Colleen's suspicions, but at the same time it estranged her from him.

Colleen had told me early on about the chicken dinner episode. In subsequent sessions she expanded on it, gradually filling in the entire grisly story behind it. It was every bit as awful as I expected.

"I was about fourteen," Colleen told me. "I was with my parents in New Mexico. And there were other adults there, too. We were all in a room and all of us were wearing red outfits."

She was looking away from me, at the diplomas on the wall.

"What was strange was that the scene was familiar. It felt as if I had been there before. I was comfortable and I knew what to do.

"Someone brought in a young Indian girl. They tied her to the table. Then some of men sexually assaulted her. She screamed and cried the whole time.

"After that, my father took her hand and tied it to some sort of special board. He picked up a machete and with a quick hack cut off four of her fingers. She screamed and screamed and then passed out. He took the knife and without any hesitation slashed her throat, collecting her blood in a pan and then putting it in a cup. They all drank from it.

"Then four of us were given the fingers and told to eat them."

She looked like she was going to be ill. Who could blame her? There was a long pause. "That's all I remember. But I know there's more. I can sense it." Colleen's eyes welled up with tears. Her head bowed, and her dark hair covered her face.

"Do you think that I could have done that?" she asked me after a while.

"I don't know. I've heard a lot of these stories, but of course there's no way to prove whether or not they really happened."

"What should we do now?" She seemed very anxious.

"I think you should let me put you in a trance so I can try to talk to your self-helper about it."

She agreed at once. I had no problem bringing out the Guardian Angel. She claimed to live in the space above

Colleen and would enter the body to talk to me. She said that she had been with her since childhood and was happy to finally find someone like me who understood her problem and could help her. She was quite cooperative, but talked in a bureaucratic manner with very little emotion, like the voice that gives you the number when you call information.

"She seems to have a fragment of a memory," I told her. "We wonder if you have more of it."

"Yes. But there might be a problem. It's the enforcers. They may not want me to tell you. And I have no control over them."

She was quiet for a moment.

"But I think it will be okay, because her father is dead, and that part of the group has probably broken up. So I think we should try."

"So then, what happened?"

"As she told you, there was this group of army officers. Her father was one of them. They were racists, involved in the deaths of several blacks in the South. They really would have liked to castrate them and hang them from trees, as they used to do there. But it was after the civil rights movement, so it had to be done in secret. They would just kill them and bury the bodies in some field. There is much more that they did, but it is too early to tell you all about it."

"What about Colleen's memory?"

"Yes, that's a relatively simple one. It was sort of an elimination ceremony."

I gave her a puzzled look.

"She was in competition for Alpha Priestess."

Another puzzled look.

"In every organization there is a competition for the top jobs. And Alpha Priestess was one of them. An Alpha Priestess is supposed to be able to take this type of horror without flinching. It was a test. And she passed, so she went on to the next level. She passed all the tests until she left. And after all the work they invested in her, they most likely want her back."

I wondered how this could be so, since she had just told me the group had probably broken up. Perhaps it was residual paranoia. And if she went through what she believed she went through, who could blame her?

"Why did she leave?"

"Her father died. Then her mother ran away with another man, leaving her with her uncle. He started to have sex with her. She was in high school then. For a while she allowed it. Then she ran away. She put herself through a few more years of school, then joined the airline."

"If her father is dead, who would be concerned that she left?"

"Well, others are still alive. And she has a lot of information about them."

"Tell me about the memory."

The Guardian Angel repeated the gruesome episode I had heard Colleen outline, filling in details here and there. Colleen, it turned out, had switched after it had started, leaving her alters to take part in the ceremony. A personality who called herself Dracula's Daughter drank the blood, naturally enough, and it was a dog personality that gnawed on the finger. During an orgy scene that followed, Carina was in control of the body. That same personality, incidentally, was the one who was the masochist.

We then fully abreacted it. It was a nasty one. There was a dog growling around on all fours, and Dracula's Daughter wanted more blood. I knew that I would have to see Arne the following day.

AFTER the abreaction Colleen was such a mess she could barely get to my office for our sessions. And she was so terrified, she would call me several times a night. Most of the time she just wanted to know I was there. Sometimes hearing my voice on the answering machine was enough.

She remained in this state for weeks. She had gone back to waitressing by this point but had to take time off from work. I was so concerned that I asked colleagues in Philadelphia about having her hospitalized. Her plight attracted much attention at meetings of the incest survivors group. Her friends would try to get her to tell her story, to get it out of her and relieve the tension. Gradually, with their help, she calmed down.

Then Colleen essentially took a break from abreactions. We spent our next sessions together discussing her family and what made them do the things she said they did. We had philosophical discussions about the nature of evil. She was trying to develop a mental framework within which to place the awful episodes.

After a few weeks of this, she started having flashes of other rituals. We would talk to her self-helper and, if necessary, abreact the episode. Then I would give her a few days to fully integrate the memory.

For a while, I felt Colleen was on the way to recovery. But the memories kept coming, and they grew more and more bizarre. She was convinced she had been used by the CIA as a prostitute to trap KGB agents. People in high places, she said, were members of her father's group. A governor. A congressman. A senator. I became more and more suspicious of her claims that she was to be the group's Alpha Priestess, designated to take over the cult. (Ever notice how most people who believe they were reincarnated are convinced they were Cleopatra or George Washington?)

I had other reasons to be wary. I was supervising several inexperienced therapists and the odd thing was, several of their patients seemed to be remembering remarkably similar traumas. One told of being abused in an amusement park. Then the next week two other therapists would report that their patients told them they were abused the same way. All three patients were members of the same chapter of a self-help support group for adult victims of child abuse. When the therapists asked them about it, two of the patients said that they heard the third tell the story and it triggered their own memory of a similar experience. They were all convinced they had been abused that way.

It reminded me of what happened a century ago when a fire occurred at the Salpêtrière hospital in France, where the famous neurologist Jean Marie Charcot was studying hysterics. While the building was being repaired, Charcot's patients were moved into the same ward as the epileptics. After a few weeks, the hysterics developed symptoms of epilepsy.

In one recent study, Doctors Frank Putnam of the National Institutes of Health; Philip Coons, a past president of the International Society for the Study of Multiple Personality and Dissociation; and Victor Milstein, professor of psychiatry at Indiana University, obtained independent verification of abuse in 17 of 20 cases of multiplicity. But there is always the possibility that patients can confabulate.

I was worried about my responsibility to my patients and my profession. Only recently had those of us treating multiplicity gained a measure of credibility. And there were still plenty of nonbelievers. False cases or exaggerated reports could greatly undermine not only our work but the recognition, which we have worked so hard to establish over the past decade, that multiple personality disorder is much more common than we had all thought.

Fortunately, the creator of this particular dilemma helped solve it. It happened after an abreaction in which Colleen re-enacted eating a stew of human parts. Her mother had kept them in a freezer in the cellar, she said. She brought them upstairs, put them in a large kettle to boil it. Then she set it on the table. Colleen looked at me with a particularly pained expression.

"I'm not sure any of this is true," she said. "That any of it really happened."

I didn't say anything. I was thinking the same thing.

"Something is wrong. What if I made the whole thing up?"

"Why would you do that?"

"I don't know. Sometimes I just think I did. But sometimes I'm sure it really happened."

It was so similar to the language that Rebecca used the first time I met her. Curiously, though, the flavor of Colleen's abreactions was different than that of Rebecca's. The emotions Rebecca was going through now triggered my own emotions. Colleen never elicited that kind of response. But then, abreactions are inherently deceptive. Usually, when a patient abreacts a memory, it feels true, both to patient and therapist. It is almost tactile, almost real. And afterward the patient generally starts to get better. Since this process is beneficial, I rarely question it. But I really don't have any evidence that the memory being abreacted is real—certainly nothing that would be admissible in a court of law. What's more, abreactions commonly occur while a patient is hypnotized, in a state in which an imagined event can be perceived as real. Contrary to what some people think, an episode remembered by a patient under hypnosis is not necessarily true.

"I really don't know how to answer you," I told Colleen. "What if it all were true? What would that mean to you?"

"That they were bastards and should be punished for what they did."

"And if none of it were true?"

"I would feel terrible for accusing them. And I suppose I would have to make up with her. My mother, I mean."

She was silent for a few moments. Then her head dropped to her chest and she started to cry softly. The tears ran down her cheeks.

"Could you give your tears a voice?" I asked her.

"What do you mean, a voice?"

"Just imagine each tear is a word that is trying to say something. Listen to it. Tell me what the tears say."

She started to cry a little louder. In between sobs, she

stammered, "She never loved me. She loved my brother, but she never loved me. She criticized everything I did. There was nothing I could do right. I tried so hard to make her love me, to accept me. I never could.

"Some days she would be nice, and I could talk to her. But then without warning she would yell at me. Or just hit me."

"Tell me more about your mother. Did she drink?"

"No. I have memories of her being nice. I have memories of her being horrible. I just don't know what is true."

"Do you think she might have switched to other personalities, like you do?"

Colleen looked like I had hit her with a brick. Her eyes had a strange look to them like she was focused inward.

"Strange that you should say that. Why didn't I remember it? I think she did switch. Her eyes would be different sometimes. One minute she would be nice, then she would turn mean, yelling and screaming. I was always in fear. I tried to be good. To get her to love me."

Then, after a pause, she continued.

"You once said that incest is a crime between three people. I've thought about that a lot. I had forgotten, but do you know what my mother used to do? She would encourage me to be with my father. To have sex with him. He was always wanting sex. He had this pornography collection. He would take me in the car with him to college campuses to look at the girls and masturbate. Or make me masturbate him. It was awful. I think she wanted to use me to keep him happy. You know, to keep him in the house, so he wouldn't rape anybody. She would tell him to bathe me when I was a child and he would abuse me in the tub. It sounds terrible, I know, but when he humiliated me, or abused me, that was really the only time I can remember that I felt my mother loved me. She would care for me afterward and tell me that I was a good girl. Such a good girl. And I was. I hate her. Why didn't she love me?"

Colleen was crying again now. Her grief seemed deeper

than when she talked about the rapes and the other abuse. I felt tears running down my own cheeks. I have often thought that abandonment by one's mother is worse than almost anything a father can do.

At the beginning of our next session, Colleen's Guardian Angel came out right away, without hypnosis.

"Catherine, the original personality, the one that was born, has something to say to you. She doesn't want to, but we told her it was absolutely necessary."

"Catherine? The one that was born?"

"Catherine was the birth personality. It was through her that all the others were created. Even Colleen. But she went away. She couldn't stand it anymore. We thought she was dead, but she's here now."

Self-helpers are supposed to know everything, but sometimes they don't tell you all of it. Or sometimes they are low-level self-helpers who do not know all of it themselves. (And sometimes, I must admit, I suspect that patients may use self-helpers to manipulate their therapists.)

Deciding not to follow the rabbit into the bush, I said I would be glad to talk to Catherine. When my patient next spoke, it was with a frail voice.

"I used to lie in bed, knowing that he would soon come in," she said. "I used to pray for my mother to save me, yet I knew she wouldn't. I can remember telling Mommy about it afterward, and she would say, 'Daddy loves you,' and tell me I should be nice to him. I didn't understand. I can remember being frightened. I can remember making up things in my mind when Daddy touched me, so I would have something to think about while he did it. I thought about stories and fairy tales. When I got older I read a lot about mythology. Greek and Norse mythology, mostly. I embellished it with my own fantasies. They let me go away in my mind while it was happening. It was the only way I could take it. It was my way to survive."

I thought about her incredibly beautiful and complicated internal world and the dizzying array of personalities.

"What about the ceremonies you remembered?"

"He was evil. He would touch me by himself. Then he would do it with some of his army friends. Once or twice they dressed up, but I guess I added to it. I'm not sure now how much happened, how much I added. It's all mixed up in my mind."

"It doesn't matter," I told her. "You were abused—that's what's important. You're just as dead if a car runs over you as you are if a train runs over you. The worst part was that the people who were supposed to take care of you didn't. So you made up stories that were worse than what happened to you. Maybe you wanted attention. Maybe you wanted to be helped, and thought that was the way to get it. And who could blame you?"

Certainly not I.

Chapter 15

THE SLASHER

I knew I would again have to violate my rule about asking the first question in the session when Randall arrived for her first appointment after the Annie abreaction. She walked in my office wearing sunglasses and with the collar on her leather jacket turned up. She had three gashes on her right cheek and another three gashes on her left. They were parallel lines, each running between her ear and mouth. Three plus three. Six.

"What happened to your face?" I said as neutrally as possible.

"I don't know. I left here feeling tired, but positive. I was a little hungry, so I decided to have dinner, even though it was a little early. I stopped in a coffee shop, got up my courage and ordered a hamburger. Rare. And it was a miracle. I was able to eat it. Then I went home and watched a little television—some movie on the cable—but I was tired and fell asleep on the couch. When I woke up it was morning. I went to the bathroom to wash my face and brush my teeth, but when I looked in the mirror I couldn't believe it. I just couldn't believe it was me. I took the day off from work. I might have to stay home until they heal.

"I keep trying to think about how it happened, but I can't remember anything except what I told you. This has happened before, the cuts I mean, but never on my face. I feel so discouraged. What good was all that work we did?"

She wasn't the only one who felt discouraged. We had carefully planned the abreaction, waited a proper amount of time, and I thought, went through it perfectly. I had expected a tired or maybe even depressed patient for a while, until everything settled down again. But I had not anticipated that Randall would have a worse outbreak of a symptom for which she had consulted me. I noticed that she still had on her leather jacket. It was not a good sign.

What went wrong? I didn't know. And I certainly didn't know what to tell her. I tried out a few lines in my mind. "Sometimes things just don't work and we have to be adult about it. . . . Psychotherapy is an art, not a science. . . . When things get worse, we know that we're on the right track." No, none of these would work. At times like this I often wished I still practiced classical psychoanalysis. Then I could just sink back in my chair and say something like, "I notice that you are upset today. Would you care to talk about it?" Or even say nothing at all. But I had a patient in front of me, waiting for an answer. I had to come up with one. I owed her one.

"I can understand your disappointment, Randall," I began. "I'm disappointed also. I really thought that we had it. It must be awful to go through all that pain and feel that it was for nothing."

"That's easy for you to say," she snapped back. "You don't have the mark of the devil on your face."

"I know it didn't happen to me, but I can imagine how bad you must be feeling."

"Stop patronizing me. Look at my face, damn you."

She was near tears.

"I see your face, Randall. I know you're upset."

"That doesn't help. You told me that we had some unfin-
ished business that we should attend to. I did what you said,
and look what it got me."

She went on like this for a while. As she talked, I felt
myself getting angry. I had tried to be empathetic. Now I
was tempted to defend myself and make her take responsibility for her actions. After all, I didn't cut her. She cut
herself.

Fortunately, I had made this mistake with enough other
patients to know that defending myself would only make
matters worse. I knew I had to change my angry thoughts
back to sympathetic thoughts, so I tried to imagine what I
would feel like if I were Randall. How would I respond if I
had gone to sleep and awoke with cuts on my face? Cuts all
the world could see. Cuts made by a part of me I could not
control.

We both sat silently, with our separate thoughts. Gradually, Randall's expression softened and I could see a tear
track down her gaunt left cheek. The atmosphere in the
room became calmer.

"I really don't know what went wrong," I told her softly,
"but I think we should try to find out. Are you willing to
undergo a little more pain? I can't promise any results."

I must have misjudged the situation and intervened too
soon, for immediately after I made my suggestion the tears
stopped and anger flushed across her face.

"Do I have a choice?" she said sarcastically.

I didn't answer. How could I? I just waited. I wanted to
make sure that she had enough time to ventilate all her
anger.

"Either they brutalize me or you brutalize me," Randall
said. "That's what my life is about, isn't it. Letting someone
brutalize me. And you know what, I'm fed up with it. I'm
fed up with not being able to control what happens inside
me. How would you like it? You go to sleep and while you
are sleeping someone else takes over your body, goes to the
bathroom, takes out a razor and cuts your face. No matter

what I do, nothing works. Nothing. What's wrong with me? Why can't I control it?

"Look, Randall," I said, "I know you're disappointed and angry that the work we did wasn't as effective as we might have wanted, but we really have to find out what went wrong."

She didn't answer. She just glared at me silently. I sat quietly and held my ground. It was up to her.

"All right," she finally said, her head dropping forward as she rested her forearms on the knees of her chinos. "At least if I keep working with you, I can tell myself I've tried to take control of the situation. But who knows? I may wake up tomorrow with an even worse face."

I moved in quickly, before she had time to change her mind.

"Why don't you take a few minutes to relax, Randall. Think about all the things that are bothering you. Think about them one by one and then put them in a large trunk that you can imagine is next to your chair. That's right. Then take the trunk, close the lid and put it outside the door to the office. Don't worry. All those things will be there for you to pick up when you leave, if you choose.

"Now, let's see if you can let yourself become a little more relaxed. Listen to your breathing, in and out, in and out. That's right. You don't have to do anything to breathe. Your body knows how to do it, all by itself. All you have to do is listen to it. See if you can feel where the air hits the inside of your nose. Where it touches the back of your throat. How far down it goes. See if you can feel it going down, deep into your lungs, and then out again, into the air. Notice the different feel between the breath that goes in and the breath that goes out. That's right. In and out, in and out. Let your breath relax you. Get as relaxed as you can, and when you are ready, let me talk to the personality who cut your face last night."

As I went through the induction I watched her eyes close and her body grow slack. Her shoulders drooped and her expression was blank. When I asked her to switch to the slasher personality, her body obediently twitched. The face sprung to life.

"You wanted to speak to me?" The tone was hostile.

"Thank you for coming out. Was it you who cut her face?"

"Didn't you ask to speak to the one who cut her face? Who did you think you were talking to, Clara Barton?"

"Sorry. I just wanted to be sure. After all, you all look alike."

"We do not look alike. Can't you tell that I'm a man?"

Obviously, this line of conversation was leading me into trouble. I was being nailed for everything I said. Probably another form of Randall's anger with me, I thought to myself.

"I thought we had a contract? I thought you agreed not to cut her?"

"The contract ran out. I didn't feel bound any longer."

I had to admit, he had a point. I had neglected to renew the earlier contract because I was sure Randall's abreaction had solved the problem. But clearly the problem was still with us.

"Can we make another contract until we figure this all out?" I pleaded.

"One was quite enough," the Slasher said coldly. "Besides, I cannot do that."

"Why not?"

"I have my instructions."

"Instructions?"

"You heard correctly."

Randall's skin was stretched tightly over her cheekbones.

"I thought you were autonomous. I didn't realize that someone else instructed you."

"We all have to answer to someone. Why shouldn't I?"

"So, you're just an instrument for someone else."

"Why are you so dense? Why can't you get it?" he said meanly.

"I guess I'm confused because you were able to make a contract with me before."

"That's right. It was their idea. I like cutting her. I especially like it when she wakes up and finds the slashes. I like surprising her that way. And this time was good, wasn't it? Six slashes. The sign of Satan. That really gets her upset."

"Why did you have to do that?" I asked.

"She deserved to be punished. That's my job."

"Why did she deserve it?"

"Are you serious? Didn't you listen to what she told you? They put people in jail for doing what she did. The Bible says, 'Thou shalt not kill.' "

Then it hit me. I had thought the incompleteness of the abreaction was the problem, and that by completing we would resolve it. But the whole abreaction only made the problem worse. Randall was cutting herself because she felt guilty. I was so caught up in the content of her memory, the drama of it, the grotesqueness of it, that I forgot the real reason for going through it—to help Randall get over her guilt for the death of Annie. Having all the feelings along with the memory provided her with even more proof that she had indeed taken a life. The abreaction was reinforcing her guilt rather than alleviating it.

In search of a better strategy, I decided to try cognitive therapy, which in my view is a fancy term for logical talk. The theory is that behavior and feelings flow from a person's beliefs, and if you can change the beliefs you can change the behavior and the emotions. My gut feeling was that she would probably resist this new technique, but at least it might buy me time to think of something else. Who knows? Maybe I would get lucky. Or she would get lucky.

"She had no choice," I told Randall's avenging alter. "If she didn't kill Annie, she would have been killed herself. She was merely the instrument for Annie's death, the same as you are the instrument for Randall's punishment. If someone shoots someone else, do we put the gun in jail? Besides, if it is proper to punish her, then you too should be punished. It's wrong to cut someone, you know."

"I am merely the instrument of others. I was just following orders."

"So was she," I said. "So did she."

"But I am on the side of justice. It is wrong to kill." Randall folded her leather-clad arms across her chest.

"But she was only a child. She didn't want to kill Annie, but she was frightened for her own life. She was doing what her parents wanted her to do. Think of it, a terrified child, subjected to extremes of deprivation and threatened with death. Don't you think you're being a little harsh? She was only a child."

"She should have known better. Even children have values."

The alter met my gaze for a moment. I noticed Randall's eyes were blinking and her thin face twitched slightly. I believed I had an opening.

"Annie would have died anyway, as well as Randall. And you know better than I how much good Randall has done fighting people who commit these crimes and taking care of the victims."

He was looking even more uncomfortable.

"What's happening to you?"

"I don't know. My eyes feel funny."

"In the corners?"

"Yes."

"Focus on your throat and chest. Do you feel anything there?"

Another pause. More blinking. Then she started to cry.

"I don't understand. What's going on?"

"It's okay. We'll talk later. For now, see if you can stay with it. Focus as much of your attention as possible on the place where you feel the emotion."

For some reason or other, he did what I suggested. Soon

more tears were welling up, and he started to sob gently.

"Please tell me what is happening to you."

"Go to hell."

The alter's burst of anger showed me that I had touched a nerve. I let the attack on me pass, since I didn't want to get into a fight.

"I know you are uncomfortable, and that's why you said that. Something I said is causing you to feel emotion, and I know that must be frightening for you."

"I am not allowed to have emotions. Never. I'm supposed to be merciless. I am told to punish her, and I do."

"It would seem otherwise."

There was no response. I paused for a minute or so. Then I looked directly in his eyes.

"You said you were simply the instrument of someone else," I said, in as sympathetic a tone as I could manage. "In reality, it hurt you to cause pain, but you had no choice. The same way she had no choice."

He sat there, crying softly. I was feeling sad also. I was thinking of the many times I felt guilty when I should not have. And of unwarranted punishments I had suffered as a child for things that were out of my control. I was thinking especially of the punishments I inflicted on myself in the form of self-recrimination. It was so needless, the time and energy I wasted criticizing myself. The time and energy most of us waste criticizing ourselves.

"I have to go now," the Slasher said, breaking the sad silence. "I need to think things over. And I promise I will not cut her anymore. Let someone else do it. I don't want that job anymore."

His eyes closed and the body slumped. Then the eyes opened and Randall was back.

"How are you feeling?" I asked, though her bewildered expression told me all I needed to know. "Do you remember what happened while you were in the trance?"

"Yes. I heard it. The whole conversation. But I don't

want to talk about it now. Isn't it time to go?" She shot her watch out from under her leather cuff and glanced at it.

"Yes. But let's meet again tomorrow, if you have time. Okay?"

"Yes. I was going to ask for an extra session. Too much has been happening to me. Besides, I have plenty of time, since as you can see I can't go to work." She dug her sunglasses out of her pocket.

"I think this will get straightened out," I told her as she left. "But for now, I want you to go home and get some rest."

I half expected Randall to come in for her next appointment bearing the evidence of more self-inflicted punishment. A burn from a cigarette, perhaps. But I noticed no additional scars. In fact, cuts that were so prominent one day earlier were already starting to heal nicely. I've always been amazed by the healing power of multiples. I once had a patient who tore her Achilles tendon, but was back running a month before the doctor expected. It makes one appreciate the control the mind can have over the body.

"Do you remember anything from yesterday?" I asked Randall, trying to ascertain if she still remembered the session or whether she had found it so upsetting that she dissociated it.

"You talked to the one who slashed me, and you upset him. He's still sulking, refusing to talk to anyone," she said flatly.

"What else do you remember?"

"There was something about him being the instrument of another one. What does that mean?"

"I'm not sure about that myself. But I suspect that you have another personality or group of personalities that were giving him orders. Is it okay with you if we look for them?"

"I guess so." She ran her thin fingers through her short blond hair.

I was able to put her into a trance quickly and got right to the point.

"Can I talk to the ones who gave the instructions for Randall's face to be cut?"

Her eyes opened and I knew I was dealing with someone with an unusually strong presence. Her chin was jutted out. Her eyes pierced like lasers. They went right through me. I felt as if she could see into my soul.

"Who are you?" I asked.

"Arachne."

"Arachne? Have I heard this name before?"

"If you are at all educated you may have. I am named after a peasant woman in a Greek myth who was a weaver."

"Tell me about her." I was looking for a way to make a connection and build rapport.

"The goddess Athena heard about her and challenged her to a weaving competition. Arachne won. Athena went into a rage and cut up Arachne's work, then beat her with the shuttle. Arachne, humiliated and angry, hanged herself. Athena felt guilty and sprinkled Arachne with a magic liquid, which brought her back to life but in the form of a spider, forever weaving webs. So that's what I do. I weave a very tight web to keep her in line."

"How?"

"Through the use of various groups."

"I'm sorry, I don't follow you."

"The groups are used to control and protect her."

Arachne volunteered little more, despite my questions. I got more glares than information. I started to think I had made a mistake by suggesting that we further investigate the slashing of Randall's face. I thought again about the advantages of being a classical analyst. I could just drift off into the silence for the rest of her 45 minutes. But I knew it would not work with this kind of patient. She had constructed a system designed to protect her at all times, especially when we were close to dredging up sensitive and painful memories.

"I'm sorry to keep pressing you," I said to Arachne, "but we have a serious situation here. We need some more information to prevent a recurrence of the slashing. If you are in charge of the groups that are designed to protect her, you should cooperate with me. I'm just trying to prevent her from being cut again."

She thought for a moment.

"The groups are part of a very intricate structure, like a spider web," she said, lifting her hands in front of her and extending her fingers as if to enclose a small globe. "They work together in various combinations to protect her, by keeping her in line. It is like an Escher painting. Are you familiar with the artist Escher?"

I nodded.

"Why does she have to be kept in line?" I asked.

"Because if she steps out of line she will be killed."

Now, she pointed a finger at me. I knew the answer, but asked the next question anyway.

"Who will kill her?"

"Most likely her mother or father. Or maybe one of the others."

"That makes sense," I said lamely, ignoring for the moment the fact that both her mother and father were dead.

"We have to anticipate every move and counter it. We have to make sure she does everything perfectly. To escape the fate of being controlled for evil ends, the child must fight back, yet appear to act completely compliant."

"How?"

"In many ways. You stumbled upon one of them. We make her feel guilty. Guilt is an effective method for controlling someone. The minute she steps out of line, we create overwhelming feelings of guilt in her."

"Making her think twice before she does anything?"

"Correct. But more than that, by creating the pain ourselves we maintain control. We can create more pain than they can, so we are in charge, rather than them. We will devastate her before they can devastate her. We will leave nothing for them to devastate. Do you remember what the Russians did during the German invasion in World War II?"

"They retreated to the interior," I said, "and as they went they destroyed their own land so the Germans would not be able to use anything they found or have the joy of destroying it."

"Exactly. And that is what we do. We always maintain control." Her voice was cold.

"Tell me about these groups. How many of them are there? What are their jobs?"

At this point, she perked up a bit, and her voice became animated.

"First there are the Hammers. They destroy any opinion she may have about any situation. Thus, she does not know what is right or wrong and has to accept our judgment.

"Then there are the Crowbars. They open her mind to let in the opinion of the others, whoever they may be.

"Next is the Tribunal. For any wrongdoing, she is brought before the Tribunal, instead of a jury of her peers. The Tribunal has ultimate absolute authority. It works in combination with other groups, including the Guilt-Makers. They are cruel and unyielding. The Precision-Makers ensure that whatever she does is done perfectly. If not, she is sent to the Tribunal, which can activate the Guilt-Makers. The Moving Standards are even more potent when they work with the Precision-Makers. She can never achieve their goal. But she must always try her hardest. And if she argues, she comes up against the Obedience Wraiths. They command her to obey. To ensure that she has no opinion of her own, there are the Fog-Bearers and the Dissolvers. And if they fail, the Atomizers take over and turn every remaining thought into a tiny droplet that is dispersed before it can form a whole thought. And if that, too, fails—or sometimes just to confuse her—there are the Ambivalent Ones, who make her change her mind every time she makes it up. You would find them interesting.

"And of course there are the Brow-Beaters, the Accusers and most important of all, the Keepers of the Bottomless Pit of Past Mistakes, who at any moment, for any reason, can dredge something up from the past and use it to batter her, or send her to the Tribunal again. And any of these groups can team up with any of the others."

Her head was drooping now. Her eyes were bleary with weariness. I was amazed. Randall's internal world was barely comprehensible, though I had to admit it had a certain logic. According to Arachne, it was all designed to ensure that she did what was asked of her, which would preserve her life in the hostile environment that Randall said was her childhood.

But what once was an effective system to preserve life now was impeding her growth. I decided to tell that to Arachne.

"You're correct," she replied. "It's a problem, which is why we're talking to you now. The system was originally set up to protect her. She had to anticipate what her parents wanted and comply to avoid punishment. She had to stay ahead of them. In fact, there are a whole group of alters whose job was to try to anticipate what her parents would think and know ahead of time what they wanted. Very often, her parents really wanted something different than what they said they wanted, so we had the Decoders as well as the Mind-Readers, the Record-Keepers, the Anticipators and the Fixers. But somehow a confusing message got into the system, something about 'thou shalt not kill.' We think it came from school or from some other people Randall knew. It wasn't supposed to get in, but it did. So there were conflicting messages, which activated the alter who cut her. We don't know what to do about this. We feel the system should be dismantled now. But we don't know how."

It was strange but somehow logical, I kept thinking to myself. I decided not to ask for the specifics of how the dissonant message got into her internal world. What was important was that she was asking me for help. She knew what the problem was. She knew what had caused it. She knew she could not do anything about it. She knew she needed me.

It was at last time to go to work. I had a plan. I would talk to representatives of each of Randall's groups, one by one, to determine how they were created and what their purpose was. I would take pains to compliment them for keeping Randall alive. I would try to avoid angering them and concentrate on winning their friendship and trust. And then I would try to convince them that they were now causing problems. I hoped they would realize it was time to back down.

This could take months, of course. But this was, after all, the patient who once told me she could eat a Buick if it was broken into small enough pieces.

Chapter 16

THE
SHE-SATAN

REBECCA's green eyes flashed, her back stiffened and her already prominent jaw jutted out a bit farther. I had seen this look before.

"They took my childhood," she said, spitting out the words and twisting one of her rings. "They tried to steal my life, for their own pleasure. They used me to make money. My body wasn't enough. They wanted my soul. But they will not win. I will regain what was mine, even if it means facing all of it, all of the horrors."

With a savage determination, she added: "I hate them."

I said nothing and in so doing allowed her to continue if she wished.

"To get free, I have to gather up all of this and put it together."

"I have to," she repeated, now playing with the clasp of her watch. "I have to, now."

I suggested that there was no hurry, reminding Rebecca that it took years to get this far and that another few months really wouldn't make any difference. It was important that we not go too fast, I said, and risk overloading her. I had learned the hard way what happens when you rip down a wall before the ceiling has been shorn up. That was the problem with Helen, and with Ned. I pushed both of them to unearth memories I believed would resolve their cases and ignored formidable resistance. Helen attacked me. Ned attacked himself.

But Rebecca would not tolerate a delay. She told me she wanted to see me every day, but if that wasn't possible then at least four times a week, instead of the current three. She had survived these experiences as a child, she argued. Did I think putting her through them now would really be worse?

I had little choice, since Rebecca said she was starting to retrieve more memories again on her own, anyway. Over the next few weeks, in fact, she did a lot of my work for me. She would spend hours at home in self-hypnotic trances, getting in touch with her internal world. She would call meetings of her Board of Directors and grill Sasha about which memories were contained in which alters. She prepared elaborate charts, mapping her entire world, alter by alter and memory by memory. And she was finding more and more new personalities all the time.

At our sessions, she would start with an outline of some episode and we would abreact it. It reminded me of her down-to-business manner when she started therapy. She led the way; I was her assistant.

During this period Rebecca filled in many blanks in her history. Her parents, her grandparents and many other relatives, she said, were part of a well-organized Satan-worshiping group. Her father, the immigration lawyer, would spend days in the genealogy room of the New York

Public Library, where he had already traced his lineage to the 13th century but wanted to push it farther back, all the way to the Druids.

Rebecca was not sure about her own lineage, however. She had heard talk that her birth was the result of the careful mating and impregnation of her mother, perhaps by the head of the cult or some visiting satanic dignitary. That would have been in keeping with what she said was the group's belief that it would be possible, through selective breeding, to re-create Satan on earth. It made me think of *Rosemary's Baby*.

Rebecca said she had been raised to be a priestess who would eventually rule the cult and choose the next high priest. But even thoroughbreds need to be trained, and Rebecca believed that her indoctrination began at birth. While still on a bottle she was convinced she was gradually accustomed to the taste of blood and human flesh. She could not remember this, of course, because newborns do not have cognitive memory. But she assumed it was so, she said, because her mother included blood in a younger sister's formula, as well as ground human flesh in her baby food.

Rebecca also assumed that she was baptized into the cult at birth, because the group's practice was to "christen" the children of members by pouring blood over them and then following that with chanting, dancing and, inevitably, an orgy. She described to me an even more bizarre "rebirth" ritual that she said occurred on her fifth birthday and was apparently intended to destroy any remnants of other religious or moral systems that might somehow have "contaminated" her. A cow's throat was cut and its stomach slit open. Rebecca was placed inside and somehow sewn into the dead animal. She was left there for what seemed to her an eternity but was probably only a few minutes. Then the leader, who she said was a physician, cut open the cow's belly and "delivered" this "born again" member, to the cheers of group members in attendance.

The next year, Rebecca said she was "married" to Satan, who took the form of the same leader, who consummated the union by raping his six-year-old child bride. She was also raped by other men. Rebecca told me her party dress was covered with blood and semen.

At periodic ceremonies, she said, she witnessed and engaged in many animal sacrifices. We relived some of these episodes in the office, including one in which she was forced to kill a rabbit by biting it in the neck, as if she was a wild beast. Gradually, she said, the rituals escalated to human sacrifice. The first time was when her father made her stab a child, an incident we had abreacted soon after she began therapy and which she now believed was some sort of initiation rite. Later, when Rebecca was a little older, she said, she performed a murder by herself, which she was told was an important step in her development as a priestess.

When I questioned her about the children killed at these rituals, she said that the cult had methods to obtain them. Some were abducted. Some were illegally imported, mostly from South America. Others were born to female members. These births were not recorded with the authorities, Rebecca said. The children were regarded simply as products of the cult. Accordingly, the cult could use them as it pleased.

Over and over, Rebecca said, she was told that her soul belonged to Satan and that she could never leave the cult. Obedience was fostered through techniques that were both simple and sophisticated. She told me about torture—including being deprived of sleep and food—that was used to break her will. If she could not endure it, she said she was told, she would be next to be killed.

Pleasure was a regular ingredient of the ceremonies she described. Rebecca said she was gently massaged and rubbed all over with oil. In theory, if you pair pleasure with a repugnant act, the latter will eventually become like the former.

Rebecca suspected that the cult also used mind-altering drugs, she said, since she was always being given injections or drinks that often made her dizzy. During one of our sessions, tiny Rebecca, who was always completely sober, switched to an alter named Katy, who was clearly under the influence of something, since she talked with a drunken slur, and would occasionally slip out of the chair and sometimes would lapse into flights of fantasy. Working with Katy reminded me of when I helped a friend who was having a bad LSD trip and thought the moon was burning through his apartment. When Rebecca took charge of the body again, she complained of having a hangover.

There were other sadistic tricks as well, or so Rebecca claimed. She told me of one ceremony in which blood was removed from her veins and replaced with blood from someone else. She was told that the "good" was being taken out and "evil" was being put in. She was given enemas and douches, too, she said, to wash the "good" out of her.

This use of drugs, along with those other techniques, could certainly enhance a cult's authority and power in the mind of a child. It wasn't hard to see how six-year-old Rebecca might come to believe she was witnessing supernatural events—people appearing, disappearing or being turned into animals—that proved the awesome power of Satan. As I listened to her, I realized that this might be an explanation for some of the more preposterous stories she and the other ritual-abuse patients were telling, especially about the multitudes of children they claimed were sacrificed.

Anyway, as described by Rebecca, the cult's strategy seemed designed to constantly reinforce the message that Satan and Satan alone could help her—even if she was continually made to suffer pain in his name. Satan had the power to torture her but also to end the torture. She saw this happen to others, such as the time she said she was forced to kill one girl and then watched as another was placed in the coffin with the victim. When the leader, who was dressed as the Devil, took the young girl out, he told her that he had saved her. Rebecca also told me the story of a teenage girl—said to be a fallen priestess—whose body was hacked into pieces and put into a coffin. Then Rebecca was put in the same coffin, the lid nailed shut and the coffin supposedly buried. She was left inside, she said, for a very long time. When they dug her up, a man dressed like a devil lifted her out of the coffin and said he had spared her.

By far Rebecca's saddest and most terrifying memory was the sacrifice of her own son, which by this point in her therapy she said she recalled in vivid detail. He was the result of a pregnancy that occurred, she told me, at the unlikely age of 13. The delivery was performed by the cult doctor in the presence of the members. The honor of biting through the umbilical cord was accorded her grandfather, and the infant was placed in Rebecca's arms. Later that night, reminiscent of Abraham being instructed to sacrifice Isaac, Rebecca said the leader told her to put the baby on the altar and sacrifice it to Satan. If what she said was true, no angel of God stayed her hand that day. Indeed, she said the heart of the child was removed and she was given the honor of returning the first piece to where it originated.

Understandably, this episode made for a brutally wrenching abreaction. Rebecca started to gag during the part where she had to swallow her baby's heart.

Rebecca's reward for this murder, aside from not being murdered herself, was praise and promotion. She was told that she had performed this crucial initiation rite with distinction. But the reward for abreacting it in my office over a decade later was a deep and prolonged depression. It was so bad I nervously suggested hospitalization, but she refused. She said no hospital could bring her baby back. I toyed with the idea of committing her, but knew that doing something against her will risked destroying the treatment alliance we had so carefully built. Anyway, I suspected that Rebecca, like Ned, could have just switched to a stable alter and gotten out. The last thing I wanted was for her to follow Ned's example. I had no choice but to wait it out. I could only rely on the strength of her character.

It was touch and go. Rebecca's spirit was clearly gone. Day after day, with her small five-foot frame looking increasingly child-like, she would come to my office and cry. Some days, it went beyond crying. It was more like wailing. And it would continue for the entire hour. Nothing I said would console her. I suggested that she try talking to her rabbi. She did, but nothing he said could console her, either.

After about three months, the depression broke and anger replaced it. I still don't know why. I certainly had nothing to do with it. But Rebecca became consumed with the desire to get even. Soon, she decided that the most effective way to accomplish this was to go public and expose them.

"Won't they kill you if you speak out?" I asked.

"If they kill me, they prove that they are guilty."

"How?"

"I found a lawyer who helps cult victims. He hasn't had much experience with Satan worshipers, but he has worked with survivors from other religious cults. He suggested that I give him a list of everybody that I know was in the group, as well as what they did. I don't know how many of them are still alive—I just gave him all the names I could think of."

I wasn't sure giving the lawyer the names would help and told her so. He would have the list, but she might be injured or even killed.

"I don't care. I might as well be dead as feel like this. Besides, what am I going to do? I can't hide forever. Someone has to speak out. They are evil. And there is no way to appease evil. It must be opposed, or it will take over everything."

Her spirit was back. She had mourned her dead child and finally found a way to recover from the loss.

I took this opportunity to ask her a question that had long puzzled me. Given all the programming to which she said she had been subjected, how did she have the strength—the resolve—to break away?

She thought for a while. Then she spoke:

"They trained me to function perfectly in the outer world, even while carrying a terrible load of pain. The priestess training, which was supposed to make me a leader of the group, gave me all the tools for acting independently. I developed executive alters who could carry out all the tasks of an adult life. They even created an alter whose job it was to make sure I did not commit suicide—unless they wanted me to. They wanted me to be outwardly normal while inwardly chained to the command. But instead, I left and refused to have any more contact with them. My system isolated their programming into particular alters, who were then carefully guarded. They could not trigger me when I would not talk to them. They took a gamble and lost. They trained me too well."

"I'M not getting any more memories," Rebecca said, quite out of the blue, at a session a few weeks later. "I don't understand it. I thought we had developed a system. That we were really making progress. But now nothing is happening."

I was aware that we had reached a plateau, but given her incredible drive, it had not particularly concerned me.

"I don't know what to tell you, Rebecca. You've been working very hard for months, having abreaction after abreaction. During all this time, you've never taken a rest. When was the last time you took a vacation? Maybe you just need a break."

She considered my words.

"I don't know. I think something else is wrong."

"What?"

"I don't think I've told you about the insomnia I've been

having, have I? After about four hours I wake up feeling like I've been in a fight, and I can't get back to sleep again."

"Are you dreaming?"

"I think so. I think that's what wakes me up. But I never remember any of the dreams."

"Have you asked your Board of Directors about them?"

"Yes, but they won't talk to me. I keep calling meetings, but no one comes. This has been happening since I got over my bad period."

"Maybe one of them will talk to me?"

"It's worth a try."

I helped her into a trance and, in a solicitous voice, asked to speak to Sasha. I sat back and waited, pleased with the efficiency of working with such a hypnotically proficient patient. Rebecca's body, which was relaxed during the induction, stiffened in that unmistakable way that signaled a switch. Her left hand rose, then suddenly grabbed her throat. Startled, she tumbled out of the chair and onto the floor.

I sat there, paralyzed with amazement, as she rolled around on my salmon-colored carpet, furiously fighting with herself. Her left hand was still at her throat, trying to choke her. Her right hand was trying to pull it off. It was "Strangelovian." She also seemed to be rapidly switching back and forth, from Rebecca to some other internal personality whose voice I didn't recognize. I debated whether to intervene but decided not to. Abreactions, to be most effective, must run their course. Therapists who step in because of their own anxiety are making a mistake. You don't stop the operation because the patient is bleeding.

I heard the alter say, "You broke your vows. The penalty is death. And I will carry it out."

"You won't," Rebecca spat out, gasping for breath.

Then the alter laughed an eerie, haunting laugh that startled Rebecca (and me). Rebecca started to recite the 23rd Psalm: "The Lord is my shepherd, I shall not want . . ."

"You can pray to any God you want," the alter growled. "I have a permanent grip on your soul. Nothing you can do will loosen it."

Rebecca continued to recite the psalm, and the alter continued to growl. When she finished, Rebecca began to pray in Hebrew. "Shema Yisrael, Adonai Elohenu, Adonai Echud." Hear, O Israel, the Lord our God, the Lord is One. It is one of the most important prayers in Judaism, proclaiming the existence of one God.

"I don't care what religion you practice," the alter said. "I am more powerful than any of them."

Then it said: "Eman yht eb dewollah nevaeh ni tra ohw rehtaf ruo!"

I would not have recognized it, except that I had heard other patients say the same thing. It was the beginning of the Lord's Prayer, backwards—"Our Father who art in heaven . . ."

Rebecca responded with another Hebrew prayer, which I didn't know.

"I call on the four crown princes of hell: Satan, the lord of fire; Lucifer, the bringer of light; Belial, the one without a master, and Leviathan, the serpent from the deep, to kill you," the alter intoned.

What I needed, I thought to myself as I watched and listened, was a mystically oriented rabbi to perform a Jewish exorcism. Or perhaps a priest. I just didn't know what to do.

Rebecca's left hand was still grabbing for her throat. Her mind was switching back and forth, the personalities now venomously cursing each other. I noticed the veins in her forehead were swelling. It was one of the most extraordinary sights I ever witnessed.

After a few moments, the right hand pinned the left hand to the floor. Her left arm became limp. Rebecca had finally quelled the internal rebellion.

"This thing was trying to kill me," she said, looking up at me.

I still didn't know what to do. I just wanted to keep contact, so I said, "Thing?"

"Yes. She was huge, a red phantasm with giant black wings. She had control of . . ."

Before she could finish, the left hand suddenly came back to life and reached again for her throat.

"I am She-Satan," the alter said. "I am not going to let you have any more memories, because they are allowing you to free yourself. I will not let you go free. You are mine. You belong to me. You cannot leave. I will kill you first."

"Shema Yisrael," Rebecca screamed back. "You are not really evil, you are merely the repository of evil. You absorbed the evil so I could exist. I can see the divine in you. I can see the divine in you."

Between the alter's growls, she repeated, over and over with chantlike regularity, "I can see the divine in you."

After a few more minutes the left arm collapsed again. I judged it was time to step in to try and take this struggle out of the spirit world and back to the real world. Rebecca was winning, but I couldn't bear much more.

"She-Satan, listen to me," I said. "You are not evil. She was exposed to so much evil that it had to be put someplace. She had to act like she was evil in order to survive. They would have killed her otherwise. You were the place she put the evil. You were the part of her that absorbed the evil. By doing this, you were able to keep her pure. You helped save her, body and soul."

The left hand relaxed. Rebecca—or maybe both of them—was crying.

"I don't know what that was about, except that it felt very real to me," she said, after a while. "How can this be possible?"

I remembered an experience I had with Toby many years ago. One night she was extremely depressed and considered killing herself by taking an overdose of pills. At the last moment, Anna, one of her adult inner personalities came out. "I fought her for control of the body," she told me later. "We were almost evenly matched. The only thing I was able to do was to get control over the right arm and wash the pills down the drain."

REBECCA told me at our next session that she had been tired and spent much of the previous weekend sleeping. In her hazy, half-conscious state she drifted in and out of a dream.

"I saw the She-Satan lying on the ground," Rebecca said, slipping a ring off and on her finger. "Off in the distance there was this light. Slowly, the light got larger and larger. Gradually, it enveloped her, all of her, so that every part was bathed in it. And as this was happening, the She-Satan was disappearing, little by little."

Rebecca had fragmented herself into many parts, allowing her to compartmentalize and isolate what she believed were the horrors of her childhood. Now she was facing those horrors again. As she accepted them into her consciousness, the need for those other personalities, those vessels of pain, was diminished. In the final step, the alters merge and the unified personality is restored. I believed that the imagery of her dream meant that the She-Satan was ready to take this step.

"I don't want evil as a part of me," Rebecca said, when I explained what I was thinking. "I want it to die, to go away."

"I don't think you should think of it as evil. It was a valuable part of you. It protected you. Look, you may have to accept some evil tendencies. We all have them. But once the alter is integrated it will not have a life of its own."

Still, I could tell the idea did not appeal to her, at least consciously. Rebecca said she preferred to rid herself of the alter through exorcism or transform it through alchemy.

"That's not possible," I argued. "There's no way to destroy a part of you. You have to accept all that you are."

She thought for a few moments, and then she nodded uncertainly.

"I guess you're right. It did allow me to survive. So, what do you want me to do?"

I put Rebecca in a trance and, using the imagery of light that she brought in through the dream, we began the merger that I hoped would begin the process of making her whole.

Chapter 17

THE OTHER
SIDE OF
THE MIRROR

"WE live on the other side of the Mirror, and those despicable subhumans we call mother and father are not our parents."

"What do you mean by the other side of the Mirror?" Rebecca tugged at a strand of red hair.

"Well, there is this Mirror. It wasn't there until recently, and we live on the other side of it."

"The other side of it?"

"Yes, that means we're not supposed to be here, and these things should not have happened to us."

I couldn't decide whether it was more like Abbott and

Costello or the Marx Brothers. It might have been funny, except that it was going on a few weeks after the integration of the She-Satan. I had expected that the case would go well after the merger, because the dissociative barriers were coming down. That Rebecca no longer had to keep these bad memories separate was a sure sign of her increased strength. Now, however, she was throwing me a curve.

I hoped I didn't show my astonishment and disappointment. Rebecca was introducing me, I realized with a shudder, to a group of personalities who she said were mirror images of all her separate alters. That meant that I had another 500 personalities to meet, to treat and eventually to integrate. And just when I thought the case was nearing completion.

Actually, it is common for a few new alters to be discovered in the last phase of treatment. This may be because the case is nearing completion and the patient, who wants to avoid the pain caused by the loss of therapy, creates additional alters to keep the sessions going. Or it may be that a patient has tested the therapist and is now secure enough to show additional, more private parts of her personality. In any event, I have come to regard these new alters, perhaps paradoxically, as a sign of success.

But 500 new personalities?

I caught myself thinking that I had stumbled across a new phenomenon: "double dissociation." Maybe I would be responsible for an entry in the psychiatric dictionary.

The real Rebecca was unclear about exactly when she discovered this mirror image. I switched back to the Mirror-Rebecca to try to solve the puzzle from another angle.

"What do you see when you look in the Mirror?" I asked her.

"Until recently, we didn't see the Mirror. But when the agony became too intense, I felt it in me. Finally, my system opened the Mirror and she saw me."

"She" must have meant the real Rebecca. But when I pressed the point, the Mirror-Rebecca insisted that she was the real Rebecca. She also suffered ritual abuse, she said, and formed multiple personalities as a defense against the horrors of her childhood. She even remembered abreacting the episodes with me. From all that she said, I assumed that both Rebecca and the Mirror-Rebecca had parallel but independent existences, until now.

Like any mirror image, Mirror-Rebecca supposedly looked exactly like Rebecca. (Of course, to me and everyone else, all the alter personalities looked like Rebecca.) The mirror image contained exactly the same set of alters but each of the reflected personalities was reversed, so that the mirrors of right-handed personalities were left-handed. I just listened to all this, trying to take it in.

"Look, the important thing is that you help get us out of here," the Mirror-Rebecca said plaintively. "We're trapped in this terrible place. We do not belong here. We belong someplace else, with our real parents."

"Are you saying that your parents are not your real parents?"

"That's right," she spit out. "Those despicable things are not my parents."

"Then who are your parents?"

"I've been trying to explain that to you. We were supposed to be some other family's daughter. A nice family. On the West Coast. Not the daughter of this terrible family, in this awful climate. There has been a terrible mistake."

Finally, I understood. Rebecca needed some other way to explain her childhood. When young Rebecca's life became too rough, even for her, even with all her regular alters, the Mirror-Rebecca allowed her to hide behind the fiction that it was not her parents who had abused her, but some other people. It was all a mistake. It should not have happened to her.

There would be no new entry in the psychiatric dictionary bearing my name. It was but another problem my patient was throwing at me. She sat there, fiddling with her watchband, just like the other Rebecca.

"Tell me about this mistake," I asked the Mirror-Rebecca.

"Well, like I said, we were supposed to be born to a nice family, but there was this mix-up and we found ourselves born to these terrible people. They were Satanists. Or they said they were Satanists. They just may have been cruel. They tortured us. They raped us. They tried to make us like them. To survive, we had to split up to handle the pain. And now you are making us relive all that pain. You are torturing us. It is a mistake. All you have to do is get us back to our real parents. We want to get out of here. Now. Please."

She looked at me with sorrowful eyes.

"You say that you are on the other side of the Mirror, and yet you see your reflection."

"Yes, but that only started recently. It really scared us when we looked over and saw ourselves. We never knew that there was a mirror. Then, all of a sudden, it was there and we saw ourselves."

"Are you sure that it was you?"

"Why wouldn't it be us?"

"Well, think about it for a moment. When you look in the Mirror, you see yourself, right?"

"Right."

"Well, you told me that *you* are on the other side of the Mirror. Therefore, you are the reflection."

I was trying to use their words to get them to see reality, or my reality, a linguistic trick.

"Don't you think that I know the difference between myself and a reflection of myself in a mirror? Don't you? Who do you see when you look in a mirror?"

Ducking the question, I continued.

"Are you adventurous? Are you willing to try a little experiment?"

"Certainly." She smiled slyly. "You're so arrogant, I'd be happy to prove you wrong."

At this point, I paused, suddenly a little unsure of my ground. I decided to seek out Rebecca's Board of Directors and ask them if they felt she was strong enough to endure what I had in mind. By this point, it was like switching channels on a television set. I was informed that it wasn't a problem. In fact, that was why the Mirror began talking to me.

Reassured, I returned to Mirror-Rebecca, who had not even noticed that I had interrupted our conversation. Dissociatives are wonderful that way.

"Reach out and touch your finger to the Mirror."

Slowly, her right index finger extended and tentatively moved in front of her. She drew it back a few inches. Then she extended it a little farther. Suddenly, she jerked the finger back and let out a cry.

"What happened?" I asked.

"It can't be. I felt something. Another finger?"

Then she fell out of the bentwood chair to the floor, her body trembling. Her cheeks were already wet with tears. I didn't have to say anything. We both understood what had happened. Normally, when you reach out to touch your reflection in a mirror, you feel cold glass. But this time, she was convinced she had felt flesh, and at that instant understood that she was the reflection and not the person. By giving her this experience, the Board of Directors had decided it was time to let her in on the truth. And that meant Rebecca's childhood—Rebecca's parents—were hers as well.

"It can't be," she said, regaining her composure as she huddled on the carpet.

"Why not?"

"Because no mother and father would do that to their daughter."

I tried to think of something to say, but nothing came to mind. I just looked at her, feeling great empathy and hoping somehow that my countenance would convey it.

"How could they do that to their daughter? I don't understand. I don't understand."

Rebecca, still on the floor, pulled her legs into her body and hugged herself tightly with her arms. It was almost as if she was trying to roll herself into a ball and disappear. Then she started to cry. She sobbed for a long time.

"You mean that I'm not real. I'm just a reflection?"

I gave her a nod.

"But I felt real. We all did."

"I know. She needed you, you know. The real Rebecca needed you. The horror was hard enough to bear without the added burden of fully accepting that it was caused by your own parents. You eased that burden for her."

"But what comes now? There isn't a need for me anymore."

"Maybe it's time for you to leave?"

"Leave? How does a reflection leave? Remove the silver backing from the Mirror?"

"Nothing as drastic as that. You could simply join her. Then you would cease being a reflection and become part of the real person."

"I don't understand. Am I not real? A reflection? A shadow is real. It comes from a person."

AT Rebecca's next session, I consulted the Board of Directors. Sasha, their spokeswoman, told me that the members had discussed the situation at length and felt merger was appropriate. They even had some recommendations on how it should be conducted. The reflection of Rebecca was to stand with her back to the real Rebecca's front, Sasha advised. Then the real Rebecca would put her arms around her reflection and the integration could take place.

I was impressed with their attention to detail. If we had merged them face to face, the reflection's left hand would have combined with Rebecca's right hand and vice versa, which might have caused problems.

"All right," I told my patient. Then I made a request to all the alters. "I want all the mirror alters to line up in front of all of the other personalities, with their backs to the others' fronts."

But before she could even get out of the chair, the Mirror-Rebecca must have pushed the real Rebecca out of the way.

"No good. No good," she yelled at me. "We're all going to die."

A case of last-minute jitters? I hoped it didn't go beyond that.

"I understand," I told her calmly. "I know you're afraid. It's natural to be afraid. But no one is going to die. You are just going back to where you came from."

"How do you know we won't die? You're going to put us into her. We will be absorbed."

"No, that's not true. We're going to blend all of you together. Look, when you mix red and blue you get purple, a different color. But there is still both red and blue in purple, right?"

"But I won't be me. We won't be us. Purple is neither blue nor red. It's purple. Something else."

I wasn't surprised by her attitude. If anything, I was surprised that it had gone so easily up until now. Integration is a touchy issue. It is like asking a nation to give up its sovereignty. In cases of especially stubborn resistance, I often recommend a political solution: the creation of a democratic governmental system, with leaders and a constitution. The alters then preserve a sense of independence through their vote. These coalitions are more workable than anarchistic chaos, but often they are only a step toward complete integration, just as the 13 sovereign colonies moved slowly and cautiously toward complete union, a process that took almost a century and a civil war.

But integration is worth the effort. The personality started as a single entity, was supposed to live as a single entity and was thrown off course only by unnatural events. It is right to correct the problem by unifying the personality again. All the patients I have helped integrate have been much happier once merged. They say they feel fuller and more rounded. They don't lose time. They have control over their lives. Their pre-integration fears of death and of "not being me" were not fulfilled. Yes, sometimes they complain of loneliness and miss their internal worlds and the escape and comfort they provided. But they live in the real world, rather than in a fantasy, and are better for it.

"I have to be honest with you," I told the Mirror-Rebecca, taking a slightly different tack. "You will and you won't be you. But no one is going to die. The real problem is that it's going to be painful, especially at first, for you to face the fact that your parents did those terrible things to you. But at some point, you'll feel better."

"You're not addressing the problem. What happens to me? To the me that I know?"

"You'll all be part of each other, rather than separate."

"I don't want to give up my separateness."

She was playing with a ring again, but I noticed that she was using the opposite hand from the one Rebecca used.

"You told me that it was uncomfortable not to be real, to be somebody's mirror image. I'm giving you a chance to become part of a real person. But to do this, you have to give up some of your separateness. It's just like when people, in order to live in a safe and organized society, form governments. They have to give up some of the freedom they had as individuals. Look, I'll help you do whatever the group wants."

"What do you mean, whatever the group wants?"

"Well, you're a member of a group that inhabits a body. It's not fair to let you alone make a choice that may have consequences for the others."

"How do I know what they want?"

"Why don't you go inside and ask them. You can take a vote."

She gave me a scowl as she closed her eyes. What was the status of her body now? I wondered. A garage without a car? Where, exactly, do alter personalities go when they go inside? I could never get a satisfactory answer to that. Toby used to say that she was in the rear of an internal world that sounded like a huge garden. She was under a bush, she said, out of sight. After that, I pretty much gave up asking such unanswerable questions.

After a few minutes, the body in front of me came to life.

"We have been defeated. The Board of Directors told us that we lost the vote. So we have to integrate."

She paused, then looked directly in my eyes.

"But before we die, please answer one question, honestly. Have our lives had any meaning?"

"Yes. Definitely. You were crucial. You allowed Rebecca to dissociate even further when it seemed that no more dissociation was possible. You allowed her not to face the ultimate horror until all of you were ready to face it. And I know that you don't believe me, but you are not going to die."

"LET's do it before I change my mind," she said glumly.

Once again I started the process, watching her tug at her red hair as she stood up, facing me.

"I want all the mirror personalities to line up with the personality you reflect, your backs to their fronts. When all of you have done that, signify by raising your right hand."

In a moment, she gave the signal.

"Now, I want the original personalities to slowly bring your arms around the reflections."

Rebecca's arms stretched out in front of her body and then came together, as if she were embracing someone.

"Good. Now bring your arms in so you are hugging yourself tightly."

Her arms moved as I had instructed. I told her that I wanted everybody inside to listen to me. Then I started telling them a story I hoped would push the process along.

"It was a very hot day. So hot that all the little drops of water that make up the ocean became separated and turned into vapor. The vapor went up and up and soon it formed a big, white, fluffy cloud. The cloud drifted with the wind and gradually moved far from the ocean. The little drops were very frightened, but soon forgot about the ocean and settled down to being part of a cloud.

"At some point the cloud passed over a high mountain range, and all of a sudden, without warning, the vapor split up and fell from the sky in the form of snowflakes and landed on the side of one of the mountains. The flakes froze into ice and stayed there for a long time. After a while they forgot where they came from and felt very comfortable being part of the ice covering the mountain.

"Then one day the weather got warmer and the snow began to melt. Little by little at first. Then more and more. The little raindrops that had been part of the ocean and then had become vapor, a cloud, a snowflake and part of an ice pack changed back to drops of water and started flowing down the mountain. Soon they were joined by more drops and formed a trickle. More drops joined and they became a stream, and even more joined and they became a river that roared down into the canyons, cutting away at the sides of the cliffs and carrying the dirt and silt along with it. Then it slowed. It went slower and slower. At some point, the little raindrops started to get a familiar feeling. The water around them had become salty. They had rejoined the sea, from which they had originally come. The long journey was over. They were home."

As I finished, Rebecca started to sob.

"It really happened to me, didn't it?" she said.

I said nothing. There was nothing to say. The reflection and the reality had become one, and now every part of Rebecca knew the awful truth—or at least what she remembered as the awful truth—of her childhood. I just sat there, listening to her cry.

AT her next session Rebecca came in and started sobbing right away. She kept it up for the whole hour. The same thing happened at the next session. And the next. And the next. It was hard for her to absorb that it really happened to her, that she had the misfortune to be born to those parents, that life was not fair, that her parents really did not love her. But she was trying. And when she finally calmed down enough for us to resume work, she introduced me to several new personalities who, as bizarre as it seems, insisted that they loved her mother anyway.

How could a daughter love a mother who not only failed to protect her from being abused but actually abused her, too? As these personalities explained it to me, there was an evil mother and a loving mother. They had not suffered any of the abuse and had only loving experiences with the mother. One told me about how the mother taught her to bake. Another told me how she would be taken shopping and allowed to buy anything she wanted. Another said her mother had taught her to read, and another recited stories she was told at bedtime. Others told me they created a fantasy mother who was always good. After all, they said, a girl needs a good mother.

These alters loved their mother perhaps as deeply as the others despised her. They could not understand how her mother could have done all those terrible things. They only knew the good mother. They only knew the loving mother. When I told them what had happened to the other alters, these new personalities did not believe me. At first I thought the only way to show them the awful side of their lives was to repeat some of the abreactions. But then I got a better idea: I set up an internal communication system, hypnotically creating television screens in each of the new alters' rooms, so the alters who had been abused could talk to those who weren't. This saved valuable therapy time.

A few weeks later, Rebecca came to my office with a shopping bag. She opened it and took out a beautiful lace veil.

"This is my mother's wedding veil," she said, spreading it out on the couch. "Antique Belgium lace. She gave it to me years ago. I'm not sure why, since I had a satanic wedding. Anyway, it represents my mother. I can almost smell her on it. I brought it in because I thought it would help me remember the feelings I have for her."

"What do you propose we do with it?"

"I thought that it would be a good idea if I tore it in half, to represent the good and bad sides of my mother. And then burn it."

"What would burning this beautiful lace accomplish?"

I wanted to make sure I knew why she wanted to do it.

"I think it would signify my letting her go. My freeing myself from her."

She was looking straight at me now, unusually composed.

A mock funeral, I thought to myself. Why not? It may have been unorthodox, but I suggested that we light the pyre in my tiled bathroom. Rebecca sat on the floor, the lace in her hands, looked at it a last time and then started to rip it in two.

"I hate you."

She tore at it some more.

"You hurt me."

She tore it a little more.

"You helped your friends rape me. You held my legs apart while my father raped me."

And some more.

"You made me a murderer. You wanted me to be a witch. You had no right to do that to me."

It was now in two pieces. She looked at them with cold eyes, then put them in an aluminum roasting pan I had found in the kitchen. She touched a match to one of the pieces and we watched as the ember became a flame and the flame issued a plume of black smoke.

"Bastard," she spat out. "Piece of filth."

As the fire spread to the second piece of lace, Rebecca started to sob. As I watched her, I felt a sadness building inside me, a sense of emptiness and imminent loss.

"Mommy. Mommy. All I ever wanted was for you to love

me. I tried to give you what you wanted. I murdered my son for you. I would have done anything you wanted, if only you would love me. Why didn't you love me?"

Gradually the fire went out and only ashes remained. I looked at them, then at her.

"What should I do with this?" she asked, pointing to the remains. Her voice trailed off.

"What would you like to do with it?"

I was hoping she wouldn't ask me to keep it. I didn't want it around my house.

"Flush it down the toilet."

And with an inglorious gurgle it was over.

Well, almost over. Over the next few weeks Rebecca had a profound reaction to this symbolic event. She was much more depressed than at any time in our therapy, even the period after she remembered the murder of her son. Most of the time she was virtually unable to function, leaving her bed only to go to temple, where she recited the mourners' prayer for her mother, or to come to my office, where she would spend her hour sobbing.

Chapter 18

REBECCA BECOMES ONE

THE witch may have died, but her ghost lived on. It haunted Rebecca in the form of about 500 personalities who remained even after the merger of the Mirror-Rebecca.

The complete integration of Rebecca into a single personality, which was now her unequivocal goal, seemed like an overwhelming task. Mergers usually take at least a therapy session and then another two weeks for a patient to recover. At that rate, Rebecca and I would be working for 20 years.

Sybil and Eve, multiples of best-seller fame, had 16 and 3 personalities respectively (although Eve underwent a second round of therapy years later in which another 22 alters were found). My first multiple patient, Toby, had 10 personalities, including herself, but five were twins. I had another patient, Lauren, with 20 alters, but she left therapy before a single integration took place.

I generally don't think about the end of therapy while I'm still in the middle of it, but in Rebecca's case I could not help wondering what she and I were going to do. My job was to help her attain her goal—a single, unified personality. But how?

The problem went beyond the time-consuming nature of the process. Integrations are also highly unpredictable. They can occur spontaneously or, as in the case of the She-Satan, nearly spontaneously. But even personalities who seem ready to integrate sometimes require a psychiatric ritual of some sort. And often alters simply refuse to consider the idea of merger, equating it with death.

I remember what happened when I tried to integrate Anna, one of Toby's personalities. Toby was Jewish, but Anna considered herself a Catholic, and so her resistance took the form of concern over what would happen to her soul if she were to merge. Anna wanted to have the last rites, but of course hadn't been baptized. Our hope was to symbolically baptize her, without disturbing Toby's afterlife. Clearly, it was tricky theologically. I consulted a priest, who consulted a bishop, who consulted an archbishop, who wrote to Rome, which in the end turned down our request for a ruling on whether a person with multiple personality disorder has one soul for each personality or one soul for the whole lot of them. All this took several months, during which Anna's resistance to integration must have diminished, because in the end we simply had the priest assure her that God would love her no matter what, and that proved sufficient.

Toby's integrations were intense and moving experiences for both of us. She felt so exhausted after them that all she could do was go to bed. She also had trouble thinking clearly and suffered from double vision that gradually sharpened, although her eyeglass prescription would change after each merger.

While gaining a new part of herself, Toby was losing an old friend. So was I, for I had worked with her alter personalities a long time and had come to love them, even though I knew they were but mental constructs. I especially remember the merger of Julia, the frail flower child. Despite my reassurance, Julia was convinced she was going to die. The only reason she agreed to integrate with Toby, she said, was because she loved me. When the time came, I held her hand and she said good-bye and peacefully closed her eyes. I was grief-stricken. The paradox of my profession is that, by helping people, I endure constant loss.

There was a profound difference between Rebecca and the other ritual abuse victims, and multiples like Toby. The abuse Rebecca and the others reported was so extensive that they had hundreds and even thousands of alters, not just 10 or 20. They weren't just split, they were, to use a term of art, "polyfragmented."

There was no way I could give the same attention to Rebecca's 500 personalities that I had given to Toby's 10. There was no way that I could get to know them as intimately as I had Toby's alters, or I suppose Dr. Cornelia Wilbur got to know Sybil's. Indeed, I had not even met many of Rebecca's alters, and only barely knew others.

Just when I was despairing of being able to help Rebecca reach her goal, the Board of Directors stepped forward. The Board had been valuable throughout the case, though, interestingly, I was not allowed access to them except through Sasha, their spokeswoman. Still, many multiples have what is known as an "internal self-helper," a part that holds their internal world together so they are not completely discombobulated in the external world, much like a conductor keeps an orchestra together.

Ralph Allison, a psychiatrist in California, was among the first to realize how helpful a self-helper can be for a therapist. Indeed, in one of his cases—as in one of mine—the self-helper assumed the role of co-therapist.

Through Sasha, the Board once again told me it had not

only decided it was time for Rebecca's alters to merge but also that it had a plan to accomplish that daunting task. Rebecca's integration would be conducted in stages. The idea was to combine groups of similar personalities into single entities, like bits of mercury that congeal into a big glob. That would bring the population of her internal world down to a manageable number. Then we would integrate each of these entities into Rebecca.

Sasha said the Board had even decided which group would go first: the children who had not been abused. These were alters who dealt with Rebecca's parents, went to school, played with other children and performed other daily activities that allowed her to have some semblance of a normal life despite the horrendous abuse she said she frequently suffered. The Board thought they would be easiest to combine. Children can be surprisingly cooperative, assuming you ask them to do something that is reasonable and have their trust. And once complete, their integration would provide an example for the other groups, which were the ones Rebecca said had borne the brunt of the cult's viciousness and had even played a part in perpetrating it. Sasha said that the Board would keep a check list of all the personalities, to make certain no one was left out.

It was a logical plan and, if it worked, would certainly save time. I scheduled an especially long session and started it off by asking the children who had not been abused to come to the front of the internal world, where they could hear me better. The children seemed agreeable, perhaps because they were anxious to meet other children.

"I want you all to lie down, get comfortable and see yourselves watching TV," I said, beginning the hypnotic induction. "On the screen is a rabbit. He is eating a carrot, a very large carrot. Watch the bunny eat the carrot. He likes the carrot. See, he is rubbing his belly. Now he is getting tired. Watch him stretch and yawn. Now he is lying down and going to sleep.

"Each of you get up. Go to the bunny, put your arms

around him and go to sleep. That's right, let the rabbit take you to sleep. When you are all in a trance let me know by wiggling the index finger of your right hand."

After a few seconds I saw the signal that the children were in a trance.

"I want all of you to stand up. Now, form a circle and move closer and closer to each other. Make the circle tighter. Closer and closer. Tighter and tighter. Now reach out and put your arms around each other. That's right, closer and closer. Hug each other tightly. See yourself blending into one child. There are no boundaries anymore. They have all dissolved, like little drops of water blending into one another. Go ahead. Let it happen.

"Now, in each of your minds I want you to see a glass jar filled with blue paint. And there is another jar with yellow paint. Now, pour some of the yellow paint and some of the blue paint into a big glass bowl. See the blue and the yellow swirling together, swirling together, slowly forming blue and yellow curls. See the swirls mix together and the colors change to green, a lovely shade of green, the color of trees and grass. Mix them well, putting together just the right amount of yellow and blue to make a green that looks like the fresh green grass of spring.

"Think of all that you can color with this green. Grass. Leaves. Trees. Plants. They are all part of the world we live in. Think how nice and restful the color green is. That's right, let yourself think of mixing yellow and blue. Watch it swirl around to make green."

And so these children became one. Or at least I assumed they became one, because Rebecca's body, which had been calm, became contorted. Her shoulders hunched forward, her head twisted to the left and strands of red hair fell in her face, which had a pained expression. Her hands opened and closed violently, as if responding to an electric shock.

I had Rebecca stay in the trance for a few more moments, just to make sure the process was complete. Then she woke up. We talked about mundane matters, such as what she was going to have for dinner. I was trying to distract her, to give her a little anesthesia. Then I sent her home.

After the integration, Rebecca felt out of sorts and had some difficulty with daily tasks such as cleaning, shopping and cooking. I knew the other mergers would be harder.

Next up were the alters who were supposed to have experienced the various tortures at the hands of her mother, her father the immigration lawyer, and the cult. The procedure was basically the same, but this time the integration released tremendous emotional energy. As the group merged, Rebecca's body spasmed in epileptic-like seizures and she screamed deafening screams. She kept it up until she passed out. Even after watching this process a hundred times, I still feel awe watching a patient put herself back together again.

As might be expected, the aftermath was worse, too. Rebecca was so weak she could not work for days. And like Toby, she developed blurred vision, perhaps signifying that additional eyes were somehow combined with hers.

It took Rebecca about two weeks to recover enough for the next group merger. I went through my routine, the integration took place, she screamed and squeezed my hand until it hurt. She had learned by this point to arrange for a taxi to take her home and to have her apartment stocked with several week's worth of food.

In this way we integrated the priestess personalities, who performed ceremonial functions for the cult; personalities, including Mary, who were sexually exploited for the cult's profit; religious alters; atheist alters; alters who absorbed—and became—evil, to protect the rest of the personalities; alters who said they liked to consume blood and flesh; alters who loved Rebecca's parents and took care of daily chores; and the rest of them. I tagged along on this lengthy process of integration, marveling at Rebecca's courage and stamina.

Then came the hard part—merging these collective personalities into Rebecca. Or at least I thought it would be the hard part, for by integrating with these personality groups she would be accepting on a deeper level what happened to her. First to go, again, were the children who were not abused. I put Rebecca into a trance and had her imagine that the children were in one of her outstretched hands while she was in the other.

"Now, slowly bring both of your hands together, clasping your fingers," I told her. "Closer and closer. Closer and closer."

Her green eyes were closed. Her face was twisted in a grimace and her red hair matted with sweat.

"Okay, Rebecca. I want you to bring both of your hands into your body right about where your solar plexus is."

Her hands moved toward her body slowly and unevenly, as if pushing through resistance. When her hands reached her midsection, she shuddered. She looked like she wanted to stop the process and come out of the trance. I wanted to stop, too. I was drained. I was exhausted. But I encouraged her to continue. Hesitantly, she did. Then she started screaming and finally collapsed. I sat there watching her. I knew she was feeling more lonely than she had ever felt before, even in the most miserable times of her childhood. I knew this because I was feeling it, too.

If anything, merging the other groups was even more traumatic, and naturally she took longer to recover from each of these mega-mergers. She would phone me many times during the evenings and simply stay on the line without saying anything. It was as if I was supposed to be able to read her mind and then say the proper thing to calm her down. I generally failed, but eventually she would calm down and we would prepare to integrate the next group.

After eight months of constant integrations all the personalities had been merged except Arlene, the Detective, Obedience and a few others, who we were able to take care of without much effort. That left the Board of Directors, which had been guiding me all along. I had been increasingly curious about how they were going to integrate. Now it was finally time to find out.

"You have done a brilliant job, Dr. Mayer," their spokeswoman, Sasha, told me, as if rewarding some junior executive with a promotion. "We congratulate you."

"Thank you. But you really deserve the credit. You saved her as a child, and you knew how to cure her. I was just your assistant."

Sasha said nothing. I broke the silence.

"I think we both should take a look and see if there are any loose ends."

"We have already done that," she said, with her customary efficiency. "It is finished. All that remains are the scars, which will heal with time."

"What about you?"

"What do you mean?"

"Well, don't you have to integrate into the personality? After all, your work is finished, too."

"We are not part of the personality," she said, without a trace of uncertainty. "We are simply executives who helped a soul in trouble."

"I don't understand."

"It does not matter. She does not need us anymore. Our job is done."

"What will happen to you?"

"We will do what a Board does when it is no longer needed. We will resign."

They thanked me again for my help, said good-bye and were gone. I haven't any idea where they went. And I never did meet the Chairman.

IT had taken Rebecca eight years, with six therapists, but at last she was no longer a multiple.

But she needed therapy, for single personality disorder. She felt like a different person, and in some ways she was. Blue and yellow do make green.

"I don't know who I am anymore," she would complain, twisting her rings. "I don't know how to be."

Her personal relationships changed as well. In the past she had been very compliant with friends. She wanted to make sure that she fit in. Now her sense of self was stronger, and she began to express opinions and take risks.

But as she began facing the world without her army of alters to help and shield her, she had to deal with disappointments and frustrations, just as we all do. She had to accept her place in the pecking order, even if it was somewhat lower than she deemed appropriate. My job was to help her adjust her grandiose expectations. Perhaps that is why we are called "shrinks."

Rebecca is now finished with therapy and back in school, studying psychology and starting research on her thesis, which is on the sexual abuser. Evidently, it is a continuation of her attempt to understand and make peace with her past.

She plans to become a therapist and help others who have been abused, as well as those who abuse.

Chapter 19

RANDALL, HELEN AND COLLEEN

INTEGRATIONS can be complicated and dramatic affairs, as was the mock funeral I staged to merge one of Toby alters. But sometimes they simply happen during the course of therapy, spontaneously and without me even realizing it. This was the case with Randall. Her dissociative barriers were melting, a result of the abreactions she had. It didn't take much effort on my part. All I did was compliment alters like Bat Girl and the Shield on their roles in protecting Randall and tell them that their work was done and that they were free to go back from where they came. The Slasher seemed to be completely laid to rest. The only tricky part was to figure out how the pieces fit into the puzzle, since it turned out that some of the alters were actually split off from other alters, not from Randall. It reminded me of a set of wooden dolls I once saw in a toy store. When you opened up each doll, there was another doll inside, and another doll inside of that and so on.

We wound up first merging Randy, Confusion, Julius and Sandra into Alice before integrating Alice into Randall. Eventually, I was able to merge the Slasher, Bat Girl, Shield, Obsidian, Many Pockets and Many Selves, although it became so complicated I had to rely on a family tree we laboriously constructed to keep it all straight.

All during this time, though, I was wondering how we would integrate the anthropomorphized groups—the Hammers, Crowbars, Guilt-Makers, Moving Standards, Precision-Makers, Obedience Wraiths, Fog-Bearers, Dissolvers, Atomizers, Ambivalent Ones, Brow-Beaters and Accusers, not to mention the Keepers of the Bottomless Pit of Past Mistakes. I mean, how does one integrate something called the Keepers of the Bottomless Pit of Past Mistakes?

As it turned out, no special strategy was required. One conversation per group was all that was needed. I would access them and show them that they had helped save Randall's life. When they saw that they had a positive impact, they just went away, never to be heard from again. It was almost too easy.

As they disappeared, Randall's personality changed. The self-mutilation and binges, which would still recur every so often, stopped once and for all. Sometimes she would feel an urge to chomp on a pencil, especially under stress, and we attended to this behaviorally, with a trick I used while working with drug and alcohol abusers. Whenever she felt the desire to consume a No. 2, she was to say the word "halt" to herself. Halt, I told her, was an acronym for hungry, angry, lonely and tired—common feelings Randall didn't realize were underlying her behavior. No hypnosis was needed. It was simply a suggestion on my part. But it worked.

As she integrated personalities, Randall gradually switched from androgynous clothing to more feminine styles, though she still wore her leather jacket. While still quite thin, she had gained 15 pounds. And by the end of her therapy, she was dating.

No longer a social worker, she is active in an organization trying to rescue abused children. Now that she is healthier, I guess she no longer finds working with children so frustrating.

HELEN'S treatment, while not exactly a failure, was not nearly as successful as Rebecca's or Randall's. I had hoped isolating the Evil One would lead to more abreactions that would be followed by integrations. But that was not to be. Her panicky phone calls to me stopped, her job became more manageable and she was able to handle those little emergencies that life constantly throws our way, such as having your car towed, with only an appropriate amount of aggravation. However, she was highly resistant to the idea of merging even a single alter personality.

Perhaps out of frustration, I pushed her hard. Too hard. Helen consciously agreed with me that we should move forward, but her unconscious balked. It expressed its disagreement through constant complaining and, all too often, missed sessions. She would offer the flimsiest of excuses, such as that she had inadvertently scheduled a dental appointment at the time she was supposed to be seeing me. Or she had to work late. Or a friend came in from out of town. I couldn't establish any therapeutic momentum. All I could do was wait for the day when she would complain that therapy was not helping her. Then I would have my opportunity. I would tell her that the reason she wasn't progressing was because she was avoiding her past.

But before I had a chance to tell her this, Helen met a man, fell in love and got married. This was her real goal all along—and no small accomplishment for someone who survived the childhood Helen described. This development, naturally, provided material for session after session, and thus served to push her past even further from us. There is an analytic rule that patients aren't supposed to make major changes in their lives during therapy. Then again, when the rule was made patients stayed in therapy an average of just six months. Anyway, Jeffrey, Helen's husband, loves her and dotes on her. Her complaining does not seem to bother him. He simply asks her what is wrong and tries to make it right. And when Helen finally got up the courage to tell him about her background, he was sympathetic and wise. He said that it made him love her even more. Far be it from me to interfere.

Helen is still married, still in therapy, still complaining and still rarely dealing with her past. At the heart of her case is a paradox: the more I pushed Helen to face her past, the more she resisted, the better adjusted she became.

What ever works, works.

COLLEEN's father had raped her. Her mother had failed to protect her and even served her up to him. But with all that, she still needed to exaggerate her abuse. Why?

Her abusive upbringing left her with an abysmally poor self-image. She thought she didn't deserve to breathe the air. She felt guilty for leaving fingerprints on doorknobs. In a desperate effort to feel better about herself, Colleen made the mistake of grabbing for the brass ring. It would all be better if she was the star of a hit Broadway play, she thought. In her darkest moments, she comforted herself by imagining that she was standing at stage center, in a spotlight, receiving a bouquet of roses after seven curtain calls. She never thought about what would happen when the lights came up and the audience left the theater.

It took years, but both Colleen and I finally culled the exaggerations from her past. Her therapy was long and tedious, and I had to maintain a delicate balance between abreacting the abuse and helping her realize that approval and even love would not help her now. Colleen's problem was that she wasn't loved enough as a child, and like many such children she thought it was her fault. There must have been something wrong with her, she believed. Otherwise, her mother would have loved her. This explained her willingness to let people abuse her as an adult.

Colleen's only option was to learn to love and nourish herself, which is no easy task. It meant ceasing to do things that would make her feel good about herself temporarily but that were, in the long run, destructive. Flying from city to city looking for a new place to live, for example, or selling herself as a professional "M." It sounds corny, but she had to give up her dreams of grandeur and do an honest day's work at a job she could feel proud of in order to start reconstituting herself. It was tough going, with little success.

Then, after struggling with these issues for years, Colleen threw me a curve. She told me she wanted to have a child. I was aghast. She still didn't trust men, nor did she have the money to raise a child as a single parent. Also, given her history, I was concerned about the kind of mother she would make.

I debated whether to talk her out of it, but realized that if I pursued the subject, I would lose a patient. So I reluctantly watched the process unfold.

Her plan was simple—she would go to bed with three men she selected on the basis of genetic excellence. None of them would know which one was the father, and of course neither would she, so she would not be able to ask for support, either financial or emotional.

The plan worked and she became pregnant. And then a remarkable change came over her. She told me that she wanted to become integrated at once, so she would not run the risk of switching in front of her child. And she went to work and one by one began merging personalities on her own. Sometimes she would arrive for a session and simply announce, "Catherine is now with me." At first I doubted her, but after we talked for a while I could tell Catherine was in fact in her. And I could even see it in Colleen's smile, which was now like Catherine's. At other times she would come in and tell me to help her with an integration.

Then at sixteen weeks Colleen had an amniocentesis and learned that the baby would be a boy. She had wanted a girl and was worried about how she would react to raising a male, which she regarded as a potential molester of women. Again, motivation saved the day. She was so convinced that the baby would be the answer to her problems that she re-evaluated her position on males. And when the child was born, she loved him, and even made some male friends of her own so the boy would have father figures.

As a result of the abreactive work, Colleen is one person now. But unfortunately her emotions are still quite unsettled. She has frequent and lengthy bouts of depression and is easily angered over incidents that would not bother most people. She tends to play the victim, which is understandable, given her childhood, and becomes discouraged easily. I am afraid she still has a lot of therapy before her.

Epilogue

I still treat whomever, for whatever ails them psychologically. I still teach. I still go sailing for a month each summer and still dream about a cruise to the South Pacific I probably will never make. But I am not the same person I was before I met Ned and Rebecca.

Not that I haven't been changed by every patient. That's what this work is about—change. They usually get better, while I hope I become more proficient and maybe even wiser. But Ned, Rebecca and the rest, more than any of the other patients I have treated in 20 years, forced me to deal with problems I never knew existed. The horror I had to work with—whether real or imagined—altered me forever. The abreactions I conducted with these patients instilled in me a profound sense of evil but, more importantly, impressed me with the ability of the human spirit to overcome it.

I had to be careful, though, not to let these patients take precedence over my other patients. This was difficult, since I often wanted to give them all the time and attention I could, in the belief that I could nurture each of them back to health. If only I could convince them to trust me, I sometimes caught myself thinking. But to try to satisfy their unquenchable needs would have completely drained me, starved the rest of my patients and caused me to fail everyone.

I also had to keep reminding myself that, in treating patients like these, I was often dealing with alter personalities, not the real thing. It was tempting to get down on the floor and play with these children, many of whom did not seem to have had much of a childhood, and so easy to forget that they were but mental constructs. I often wanted to hold and comfort them when they were hurting or to cut an abreaction off prematurely because they couldn't stand the pain. And, yes, it was scary to face the "evil" personalities and those who were still loyal to their abusers and would threaten me or my family. It was terrifying to think that there might be cults out there that have killed—and that might attack me because I was helping former members and victims. Part of me wished my patients were making it all up. But another part of me wanted to play avenger.

Should I have sounded the alarm? Notified the authorities? I don't think so. For one thing, the authorities have already been notified. For another, I am not a policeman. I am a therapist. My job is to help my patients make peace with what they said happened to them, not to go on crusades against the people they say mistreated them.

Well, were all their stories true? I still don't know, even though knowing would be a great help. But like Helen, I long ago took the precaution of depositing records of the people with whom I have worked with an attorney, on the assumption that the last thing any cult wants is notoriety.

It's not that I didn't try to find out. I read all the literature I could find, both professional and popular. I talked to police officers and an agent of the Federal Bureau of Investigation, who told me that they get many reports of Satanic abuse and conduct many investigations. Some agencies have even compiled lists of warning signs for parents of teenage children. And, of course, I consulted my colleagues. No one could really help me. In fact, many of my fellow therapists were in the same quandary. They were confronting an increasing number of patients claiming to be survivors of satanic cults, but they lacked evidence that these groups actually existed.

I've tossed the arguments around in my mind over and over, as have countless others in my profession, in an internal debate that has lasted years and may go on for as long as I treat such patients.

"The number of babies killed in the accounts of survivors is far larger than even the most extreme estimates of missing children allow."

"Patients say they were kept by cults as breeders, and the births of their children were not recorded. Other babies were illegally imported from third-world countries."

"If so many children were killed, why have we not found more remains?"

"They were cremated or dissolved in acid or even consumed in cannibalistic rites."

"But advanced forensic techniques would have found something—a drop of blood, a snippet of hair—some evidence that the groups existed and killed."

"The Satanists are extremely careful, and besides, sites have been found with symbols, axes, thrones and altars on which sacrifices may have taken place."

"It could be the work of dabblers and dilettantes. There's no proof anyone was killed."

"There are so many patients all over the country telling therapists they have endured ritual abuse, and their reports are remarkably similar even though the patients have not had contact with each other."

"But they are psychiatric patients. Can they be trusted to tell the truth? Aren't most of their stories retrieved in a hypnotic state, when they are impressionable and likely to exaggerate?"

"Many are highly educated, with professional degrees and respected jobs. Some have testified as expert witnesses in child abuse cases. And what about the bodies found in Matamoros and Toledo?"

"Isolated cases."

"You can go to the Yellow Pages and find the addresses of satanic churches."

"These are legitimate, legal religious groups, protected by the Constitution. Their members vehemently deny holding sacrificial rituals or torturing anyone."

"The stories these patients tell are so terrible that many people—therapists included—have to deny them in order to maintain a belief that the world is a safe and rational place."

"On the contrary. The therapists treating these patients have an investment in believing them. There are conferences and training seminars on the subject. And anyway, these patients are doubtless more interesting than typical neurotics. It's understandable that some therapists would suspend critical judgment."

Some believe the wave of ritual-abuse reports began only after the publication in 1980 of *Michelle Remembers*, in which Michelle Smith and her psychiatrist and later husband, Lawrence Pazder, tell of her escape from a satanic cult. They say it triggered "copy cat" accounts many of which were unquestioningly accepted by inexperienced therapists.

Lately, though, concern about the increasing number of ritual-abuse patients and the veracity of their stories is building, as is evident from a string of articles in the official journal of the multiple personality disorder field, *Dissociation*.

In the March 1989 issue, for example, Sally Hill, a social worker, and Jean Goodwin, a psychiatrist, discuss the similarity between the patients' accounts of ritual abuse and the historical accounts of Satanism, a congruence they argue will "assist clinicians in considering as one possibility that such a patient is describing fragmented or partially dissociated memories of actual events." They also argue that skepticism over these reports could be because therapists lack a framework "within which such frightening and often fragmentary images can be assembled, organized and understood."

However, they cautiously add: "Until we obtain more information from those orchestrating satanic rituals, we cannot be certain to what extent accounts by observers either in historical or clinical contexts represent witnessed sadistic sexual practices, including homicides, witnessed awe-inspiring theatrical simulations, the effects of drug use and hypnosis or some combination of all of these and other perceptions."

The following December, Dr. Richard Kluft of the Institute of Pennsylvania Hospital and Temple University School of Medicine, the editor-in-chief of *Dissociation*, noted that "clinicians and scientific investigators in the field of the dissociative disorders have become quite concerned, often conflicted, and on occasion frankly polarized over the subject of ritual abuse. It is difficult indeed to know what to make of such accounts, because there is little hard data upon which to rely, and because, in my opinion, forceful and ostensibly authoritative but grossly irresponsible statements on the basis of inadequate information and documentation have been made in both the media and in scientific forums both by those who are firmly convinced that such accounts are credible, and by those who believe them to be confabulations and/or utter nonsense. I include clinicians, scientific investigators, and law enforcement officials in this indictment."

Given the lack of evidence, he, too, advises caution. "It is understandable albeit unfortunate that many years may pass before we are able to understand patients' allegations of ritual abuse as well as we understand their accounts of incest and more familiar abuses and exploitations."

Three months later, Susan C. Van Benschoten, a registered nurse and graduate student in clinical psychology at Georgia State University, writing in *Dissociation*, urged professionals to "remain open to the possibility that satanic ritual abuse does occur. . . . To realize the danger in not taking patients' accounts of satanic abuse seriously, one only has to consider instances in which reports of atrocities were initially denied and later found to be true."

Experienced and respected clinicians have noted that there is an intensity, a consistency, an authenticity to the memories at least some of these patients report. Dr. Bennett Braun, Program Director of the Dissociative Disorders Unit, Rush- Presbyterian St. Luke's Medical Center in Chicago, says that he once heard a five-year-old describe in detail what it was like to cut into a living person. "I'm a surgeon," he said afterward. "The kid's right."

But Kenneth Lanning, a supervisory special agent in the Behavioral Science Unit at the FBI Academy in Quantico, Virginia, has reviewed hundreds of reports of ritual behavior and says: "There is not a shred of evidence. There are no bodies and there is not one conviction." Lanning allows, however, that there may at least be some elements of truth to some of the accounts.

In 1990, about 20 children were removed from their homes and their families in Rochdale, England, near Manchester, and made temporary wards of the court after a six-year-old boy told social workers about babies being stabbed and sheep being mutilated in satanic ceremonies. Children were also said to have been drugged.

Subsequent news accounts reported that there had been other ritual-abuse investigations involving hundreds of children in nearby towns. And in Manchester itself, children led social workers to a complex of limestone tunnels in a cemetery where the children said they had been abused and degraded in satanic rites. Inside the dank vaults, the authorities found something that looked like a small altar, as well as crosses cut into the stone and traces of wax that suggested candles had been used. "We leave our clothes here," one child reportedly said at an entrance to the secret tunnels.

"The abuse the children describe is real and not the

product of their imaginations," the director of Rochdale's social service agency was quoted as saying. Even before the Rochdale case, in fact, the National Society for the Prevention of Cruelty to Children warned that "organized" abuse—including ritual abuse—was on the rise in England.

But to others it was far from clear what, if anything, had happened to the children. And with little evidence to go on, the authorities in Rochdale decided not to prosecute the case criminally, which one town official said was all "a horrendous mistake."

As Dr. Kluft told the latest conference on the Study of Multiple Personality and Dissociative States, which focused on the issue of the veracity of ritual-abuse reports: "I have yet to be convinced that they exist, nor have I been convinced that they do not."

It isn't hard to see how abuse inflicted on a child, who also may have been drugged, could be magnified or embellished into stories of bizarre rituals. Children's minds are full of fantasies. Reports of cult abuse could also be metaphoric projections of internalized anger. Thus, bad people become devils.

In some cases, the stories could be an unfortunate result of the interplay of pathologies. Dr. George Ganaway, clinical assistant professor of psychiatry at the Emory University and Morehouse Schools of Medicine and director of the Ridgeview Center for Dissociative Disorders, recently told me about a patient who had been treated for multiple personality disorder. The suspected cause was an abusive grandmother who reportedly had the nasty habit of inserting birds and other objects in the patient's vagina while reciting the Bible. Years later, the patient became pregnant and suffered renewed symptoms of multiplicity when the movement of her baby reminded her of the past abuse. She re-entered treatment with another therapist who had just returned from a workshop on satanic abuse. Using hypnosis, the therapist began asking leading questions and the patient, who needed to please her, was soon talking about being ritually tortured by a group of people wearing ceremonial robes. Later, when the patient began to challenge the validity of these satanic memories, the therapist told her that she was endangering her life and that of her child. Finally, she changed therapists. Without the continued reinforcement, the satanic memories evaporated in short order. In a six-month follow-up, the patient failed to have any further memories of the cult.

"Unless scientifically documented proof is forthcoming, patients and therapists who validate and publicly defend the unsubstantiated veracity of these reports may find themselves developing into a cult of their own, validating each other's belief systems while ignoring, and being ignored by, the scientific and psychotherapeutic community at large," Dr. Ganaway warns.

I don't know how to explain why so many patients are reporting similar stories now. I do not believe there is a nationwide network of satanists that reaches into the highest levels of government, commerce and culture. Yet I do not have a problem believing that some people have been abused by people who practice Satanism. Evil exists in the most extreme forms, as the Holocaust demonstrated half a century ago. And, as we are only recently discovering, there is a shocking amount of child abuse in our culture. So I try to keep an open mind, listen to my patients and help them any way I can.

IT is a beautiful August day. My sailboat, its mast repaired and its leaks plugged, is anchored just off a bend in the Connecticut River. I was waiting to rendezvous with *Yankee*, a sister ship owned by a friend of mine, Dave Wordell.

Over cocktails, Dave and I exchange horror stories about commissioning our boats, which came from the same yard in Taiwan. Dave suggests that we take a short expedition to nearby Selden Island. We agree, and soon we are walking single file along a narrow path. Dave knows a lot about the island. He gives talks all over the state about it. It is famous for supplying the stones used to build New York City's brownstones.

The path follows a small stream. We walk along, swatting at the bugs and talking about our boats. We head around a bend and come to a little clearing, where I see two throne-like chairs built from piles of stone. On each seat is a large cross constructed of branches. Nearby is a flat table, also built of stone. An altar? I think to myself.

"There have been stories about devil worship around here," Dave tells me, unaware of my interest in the subject. "I think this may be one of the places where they do it. My son and I found it a few years ago. We put the crosses up, and since then no one has used it."

I stare at the little scene for a few moments. Then I follow Dave back into the woods.